```
PN              Johnson, Robert E.
2287
.C632           Bill Cosby, in words
J63                and pictures
1986x
792.2028 C
```

**SSCC - GILL'**

Memphis and Shelby
County Public Library and
Information Center

For the Residents
of
Memphis and Shelby County

$12.95

ISBN: 0-87485-084-3

EBONY/JET SPECIAL ISSUE

# BILL COSBY:
## IN WORDS AND PICTURES

By Robert E. Johnson
*Associate Publisher/JET*

Ⓙ©Johnson Publishing Company, Inc.   Chicago 1986

Copyright © 1986
Johnson Publishing Company, Inc.
Chicago, Illinois

All rights reserved. No part of this publication may be reproduced or transmitted in any form or by any means, electronic or mechanical, including photocopy, recording, or any information storage and retrieval system, without permission in writing from the publisher.

TEXT 12/14 HELVETICA w/48 PT. CAP
RAG RHT., CAPTION 9/10 DESIGN NLH

Library of Congress Cataloging in Publication Date
ISBN: 0-87485-084-3
Printed in USA

## Publisher's Note

**B**ill Cosby: In Words And Pictures is a tribute publication to a Black man who was born of ordinary circumstance and became an extraordinary achiever. His success in the field of entertainment transcends all races except the human race.

In his night club comedy routine, he tells stories of great men and women who were not expected to amount to very much in life. But when they achieved greatness, those who foresaw failure would exclaim, as Cosby said in the case of George Washington, America's first president: "I didn't know that you were going to be THE George Washington!"

When the editors of EBONY and JET magazines discovered Bill Cosby as a budding comedian more than two decades ago, they must have had a hunch that some day he would be THE Bill Cosby!

Our editors began recording his words and pictures early in his career. Our photo files and research library reflect what Cosby has been thinking, doing, saying, feeling and demanding of himself, his family, friends, associates, organizations and worthy causes.

We are proud that Cosby began his third season with the top-rated show in television. There is more to Cosby than meets the eye on TV. So we decided to let you meet THE Bill Cosby!

This inaugural EBONY/JET Special Issue is not an authorized words-and-pictures biography of Bill Cosby, star and creator of *The Cosby Show,* which was winner of the 1984-85 Emmy Award as Best Comedy Series and the top-rated show on television for two seasons.

However, it was done with respect and care by Johnson Publishing Company's Book Division and the many people who will be noted in grateful acknowledgement at the conclusion of this special issue—*Bill Cosby: In Words And Pictures.*

**John H. Johnson**

*F*or my publisher, John H. Johnson

*F*or my wife Nemi; daughters, Bobbye LaVerne; and Attorney Janet Johnson-Vinion; son, Robert III; grandson, Cole Johnson-Vinion; granddaughter, Chloe Johnson-Vinion; son-in-law, Ronald Vinion; and all my friends who often asked, "Bob, when are you going to write a book?"

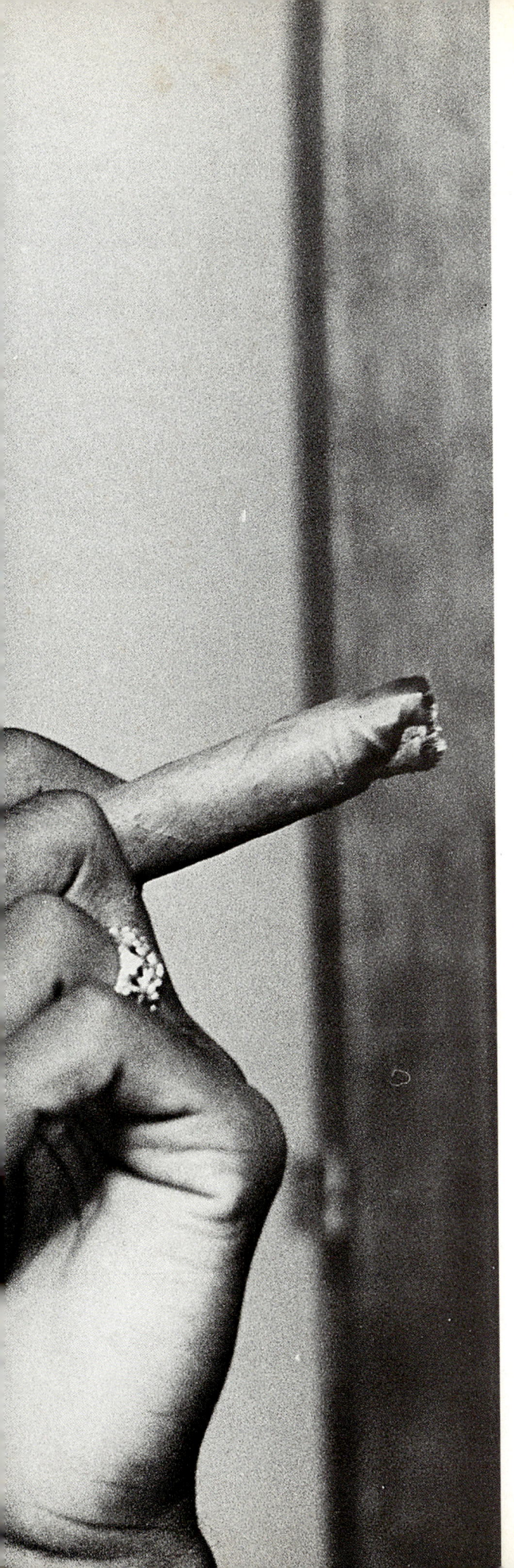

# In Words

For a man who answers to the name of Dr. William Henry Cosby Jr. in college circles and is known as multi-talented multi-millionaire Bill Cosby in show business circles, it was an incident he will always remember.

Interviewed by this writer after he had lunch with the editors of JET and EBONY magazines in the 11-story, marble front headquarters of Johnson Publishing Company in downtown Chicago, Cosby recalled the 1981 incident as if it were etched in stone and deposited in his memory bank.

"I stepped on this waitress' heel and I put my hands on her hips. I said, 'Oh, I'm sorry.' The lady said, 'Take your hands off me!' And I said, 'What did you say?' She replied: 'I said take your hands off me.'

"I said, and now very loud, 'What is your name? Just tell me what is your name.' She said, 'I don't have to tell you my name.'

"First of all, I said, 'I stepped on your heel and I touched you to steady you because I was tripping. It seems to me that you have a problem. What is your name?

"Now, the manager comes over and asks, 'Mr. Cosby, what seems to be the trouble?' I said, 'You have here a lady —if that is what she is—who seems to have a problem if somebody touches her after they have stepped on her heel and they have said I'm sorry. Now, we have here some twelve hundred people in this convention staying in this hotel. Now, if this woman has a problem, perhaps, you better put her away until we're gone because some people may not be as nice about this—' and I'm talking as loud as I can talk.

11

*Bill Cosby: Funny Faces Fueled Fantastic Financial Flow For Famous Funnyman/Father*

*Celebrating at a preview party of the film, Dirty Dozens, which stars actor Jim Brown in 1967, Cosby dances with wife Camille.*

*The celebrated entertainer's mother Anna Pearl Cosby cheerfully entertains granddaughter, Erika, during a playful moment in 1966.*

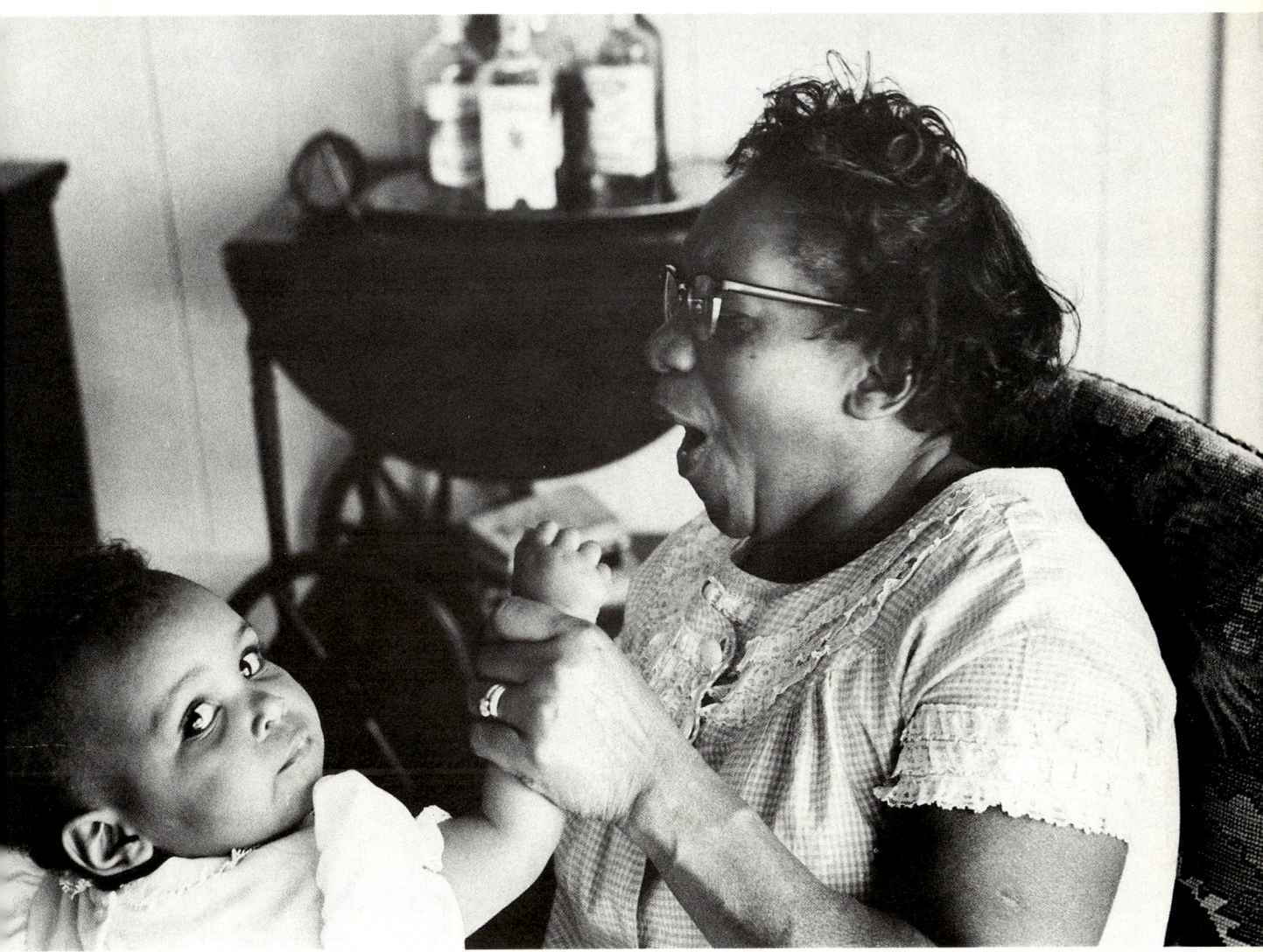

"The manager took her aside and I heard her say, 'Well, I thought he was just another nigger. I didn't know he was Bill Cosby!' "I mean the words came out of her mouth!" Cosby exclaimed.

But consider this. At the time the waitress thought "he was just another nigger," Bill Cosby was a consumate comedian, an acclaimed actor, able author, enthusiastic educator, a philosopher/philanthropist, fastidious father and faithful family man.

In his climb up the stairway to stardom, he earned a bachelor's degree in sociology from Temple University, a master's degree and a doctorate degree in education from the University of Massachusetts. The comic genius recorded 18 comedy albums, three musical LPs which sold more than 11 million copies; won eight Grammy Awards for comedy albums; collected three Emmy Awards; and starred in six TV shows and eight movies.

Moreover, at the time the waitress was characterizing him, Cosby was 44 years removed from his birthplace in a Black ghetto where it was commonplace for him and others there to be thought of as "niggers" by people like her.

Born the first of three sons to William Henry and Anna Cosby in Philadelphia on July 12, 1937, Cosby's astrological sign is Cancer. Persons born on this date are considered helpful, compassionate, sensitive, conscientious and patient.

One astrologer observes: "Cancer, who takes pride in maintaining strong family ties, it's your nature to ask 'how mother is doing?' Your concern for others and their feelings is a strong part of your makeup. With the moon as your ruler, you can't help being a romantic. Born under this water sign, while you're prone to taking action, it usually centers on doing something for someone else. Quick to say 'I feel,' others usually know what it is before you finish the sentence. If one fault is brought to the forefront, yours would be meddling others' business. Everyone doesn't plan for the future, or care about it as you."

When Bill Cosby first saw the light of day in The City of Brotherly Love's Germantown Hospital, he brought joy to the hearts of his parents who had been sweethearts since they were enrolled in the public schools of Virginia. But if Cosby's babyhood recollections are reliable, his father took one look at his funny face and couldn't stop laughing. The young couple had married and moved North in search of better opportunities. With only a public school education and few useful skills for the industrial North, Bill's young father entered the labor market. He was willing to settle for any kind of job, no matter if the work was hot, hard and heavy or he had to lift, push, pull or tote.

In the year 1937 when Cosby was born, segregation was a way of life in the South, and Negroes were mostly

*Cuddlesome Camille and Bill Cosby climaxed courtship with matrimony on January 25, 1964 while she was still a student at the University of Maryland.*

*Fifteen months after their marriage, Erika Ranee was born on April 8, 1965. The proud parents posed with their delightful daughter who brought them great joy and satisfaction.*

*In 1969, Bill and Camille Cosby posed with (left to right) Erika Ranee, Ennis William and Errin Chalene in first family photo for EBONY and JET magazines.*

As a faithful father and family man, Cosby found time in his busy career to spend time with his children. Cosby's doting mother Anna Cosby hardly had time to spoil them as a grandmother whenever her son was home. He enjoyed taking them for a ride in his choice of one of many family cars.

*Cosby kisses his first-born son, Ennis William, whose birthdate is April 15, 1969. During the year of 1969, Cosby won an Emmy Award for The First Bill Cosby Special and a Grammy Award for the Best Comedy Album, Bill Cosby: Sports.*

When he could not get a major motion picture company to produce his movie, Man And Boy, in 1972, Bill Cosby invested his money in the film that cast George Spell as his son. Cosby played role of Caleb in the family western.

In 1977, Bill and Camille Cosby posed with their happy family for EBONY (June 1977). Their children are (top, left to right) Erika Ranee, 12; Errin Chalene, 10; Ennis William, 8; (seated, left to right) Ensa Camille, 4; and Evin Harrah, 7 months.

confined to racial ghettos in the North.

In that year—four years before Japan bombed U.S. Navy ships in Pearl Harbor, triggering a war that provoked a rebirth of the Navy in which both Bill Cosby and his father would eventually enlist at separate times—Negroes were high on hopes. Some dreams were fulfilled. That year, 1937, Joe Louis defeated James J. Braddock for the heavyweight boxing championship. That feat fostered pride of race in comedians-to-be Redd Foxx, who was 15, and Nipsey Russell, 13. Flip Wilson was 4. Moms Mabley was 40. Richard Pryor and Eddie Murphy had not been born.

The year 1937 that witnessed the birth of Bill Cosby also witnessed Harvard-trained William Hastie become the first Black federal judge. Because of his anti-lynching campaign as secretary of the NAACP, Walter White won the coveted Spingarn Medal, which Cosby was destined to receive 48 years later.

In 1937, jazz was king and the juke box hit was the song *Caravan*, co-composed by bandleader Duke Ellington and his valve trombonist Juan Tizol. Paul Robeson had become so famous championing the causes of Black Americans that his platform extended overseas. On June 24, 1937, less than a month before Cosby's July 12 birthdate, Robeson made headlines with his speech, "The Artist Must Take Sides," at Royal Albert Hall in London. Black performers that year saw White performers like Al Jolson and Eddie Cantor paint their faces Black and do comedy routines. The hit radio show in 1937 was still *Amos 'n' Andy,* a creation of two White men who made use of dialect, ridiculing Blacks.

This was the climate in which William Henry Cosby Sr. began his role as a breadwinner for his new-born son in 1937.

With his earnings as a laborer, working a variety of jobs, including a welder, William Cosby Sr. was able to keep his family above the poverty level. It was in this climate that the Cosby clan increased. The second child, James, who was born two years after little Bill, died six years later, a victim of rheumatic fever.

For the next three and a half years, Bill was the only child. In his night club act, Cosby illegitimately extends a fact as he jokes: "I was the only child for seven years...My mother comes up to me one day and I was reading a comic book and cooling it. She said, 'You are going to have a little brother or sister,' and I said, why? You aren't satisfied with my work? I'll make improvements for you. What are you having other people in the house for?" Then came Russell. The next arrival was Robert. As the family increased, the father had a difficult time making a comfortable living. Things went from bad to worse and they were forced to move. Their new mailing address was in the lower-income Richard Allen Homes, a

25

*On an athletic scholarship at Temple University, Bill Cosby excelled in track events, including discus throwing.*

Cosby won high-jump events, but his football prowess caused him to be inducted into the Temple Hall of Fame in 1984.

Two decades ago, Bill Cosby and Sammy Davis Jr. shared a billing in Los Angeles. In 1986 they teamed for a night club act titled Two Friends and became a hit duo.

public housing project named for pioneer Black leader Richard Allen, who protested church segregation, founded the African Methodist Espiscopal (AME) church and became its first bishop in 1816.

He jokes about growing up there in his video titled *Bill Cosby Himself.* He muses:

"Fathers are altogether different. I'm not saying they're better. I'm saying they're different. See, my father established our relationship when I was seven years old. He looked at me and said, 'You see, I brought you into this world and I'll take you out. And it don't make no difference to me because I'll make another just like you...

"And because of my father, between the ages of seven and fifteen, I thought my name was Jesus Christ. And my brother, Russell, thought his name was Damnit.

"'Damnit, will you stop all that noise! Jesus Christ, sit down!' One day, I was playing in the rain and my father said, 'Damnit, will you get in here?' I said, 'dad, my name is Jesus Christ,'"

Economic depression, social strains and family stresses clobbered the Cosbys, resulting in a decision by the father to leave his family and join the U.S. Navy.

Growing up without a father as the chief breadwinner not only meant that the mother would be forced to find work outside the home, it also meant that young Bill's family role would increase. Not only would he have to look after his brothers, Russell and Robert, he had to further divide his time hustling odd jobs to help make ends meet — and still find time for school.

How all of this affected him mentally, morally, physically and spiritually can best be gleaned in some of his comedy albums, including *I Started Out As Child, Revenge* and *To Russell, My Brother Whom I Slept With.* Each won a Grammy Award for Best Comedy LP.

If Cosby's childhood years left any scars, he never shows them. His creative mind and comedic talent are too busy finding the humorous side of every experience he had at home, school, at work and at play.

At Wister Elementary school, Cosby had pals who would one day become Fat Albert, Old Weird Harold, Dumb Donald, Rudy, Mushmouth Nolan and Weasel — all of them preserved for posterity in Cosby's TV cartoons.

If his mind had wandered through his books absorbing the lessons with the same intensity that he wandered through his neighborhood surroundings soaking up what his parent and teachers would call a lot of nonsense, Cosby would easily have topped his class in grades.

He had a sixth grade teacher who said as much when she wrote on his report card a prophetic observation: "William is a boy's boy, an all-around fellow, and he should grow up to do

*Appearing at a record shop in Los Angeles, Bill Cosby gives autograph while promoting his record album.*

great things."

At Central High School for boys, where most of the students graduated and pursued a college education, Cosby charmed his teachers but flunked his classroom studies. His athletic exploits, he had envisioned, would be his ticket out of the ghetto into the money sports. The problem was that he wasn't fairing too well in his athletic endeavors. He recalls his high school athletic efforts with typical humor. "I was on the ninth grade football team which was made up of me and ten other guys from the remedial gym class. All we had to do was look at the parallel bars and they gave us a 'D'. I never got into the game, and I had to give my jersey to the guy who'd had his ripped."

Dismayed and disappointed that he flunked nearly all of his 10th grade subjects, Cosby tried to make up by repeating the grade. He wasn't doing much better and left Central for Germantown High School in the neighborhood where he was born.

Although his studies still suffered from neglect, his sports prospered from attention. Football and track were his specialties. By the time he was 19, he had scored more track victories than passing grades. His age then barred him from further sports competition and his grades didn't qualify him for graduation. So he decided to follow in his father's footsteps. He joined the post World War II Navy in 1956 to see

*Bill Cosby, cast as the tennis-playing secret agent Alexander Scott, rides with Robert Culp, in role of secret agent Kelly Robinson, during the filming of an episode of I Spy, which opened the door to success for Cosby in television.*

The first Black actor to land a starring role as co-partner of a White actor on network television, Bill Cosby made the transition from a comedian to a dramatic actor with the help of co-star Robert Culp. The comedian-turned-actor won three consecutive Emmy Awards before the I Spy series ended in 1968.

*In a dramatic segment from* I Spy, *Bill Cosby's female interest is singer Eartha Kitt, who had become a talented actress. He had complained that he wanted to hold more than a tennis racquet in the TV series.*

the world.

It was during his four years of enlistment in the Navy and the foreign travels that he was finally able to hear clearly the advice that his mother had always tried to give him: "Son, get an education so you will have something to fall back upon."

Before he finished his hitch in naval service, he earned his high school diploma through a correspondence course. After he received an honorable discharge from the U.S. Navy, he enrolled at Philadelphia's Temple University in September, 1960, on an athletic scholarship. At age 23, the

*After persuading the producers of* I Spy *to let him have a love interest on the show, Cosby chose singer Nancy Wilson, who was an aspiring actress and talented thespian.*

Cosby also cast another romantic interest, singer/actress Barbara McNair, who reads JET on film set. With them is Diahan Williams. Actor Robert Culp meets actress Cicely Tyson, another Cosby choice for I Spy.

In Beverly Hills, Cosby greets actor Robert Culp's new bride, actress France Nuyen. The 1967 marriage of Cosby's co-star was performed during a civil ceremony after a segment of the I Spy series was filmed.

*Sitting in the library room of his Los Angeles home in 1969, Cosby's daughters Erika, and Erinn (right), greet Sheldon Leonard, who helped Cosby land starring role on I Spy TV series.*

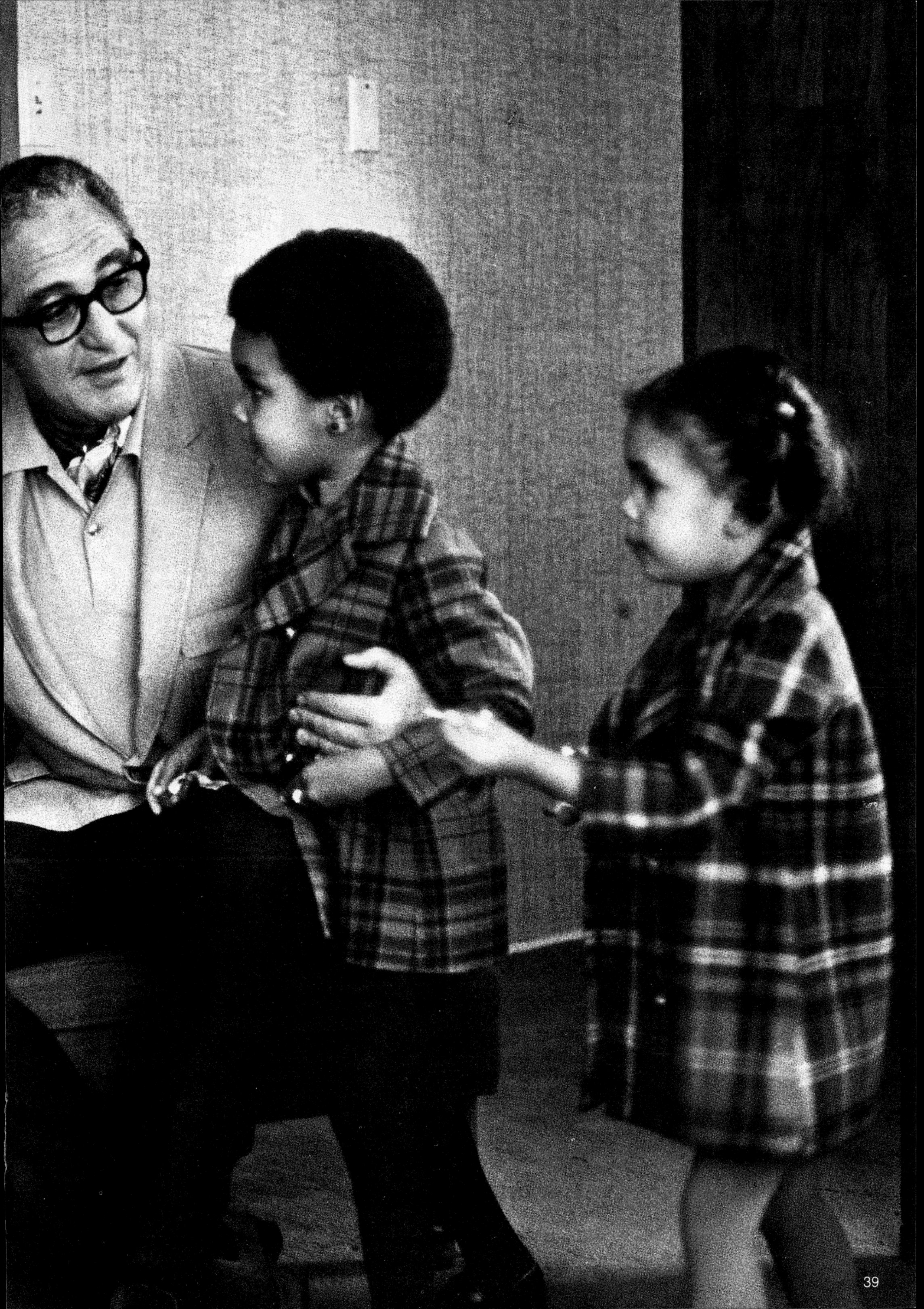

*In his Los Angeles office in 1971, Cosby sits at desk, puffs a cigar and takes a nostalgic look at photos of his wife Camille, who is a constant source of inspiration and is helpmate in his show business endeavors. He works late in office alone.*

*During the 1971 photo session for an EBONY story, Cosby is shown conferring (above) with Del Shields, assistant to the producer, at Jemmin. Cosby confers (below) with his brothers, Bob (left) and Russell, who served as production assistants on the staff of Jemmin.*

freshman student participated in basketball, football and track.

Unlike his sophomore year in high school, Cosby's second year at Temple was like being on a merry-go-round of success in academics and athletics. About all he needed was to have some walking around money in his pockets when he dated campus beauties. Then a funny thing happened when he got a job as a bartender. Located in a basement, the bar was called The Underground and the job paid him $5 a night plus tips. A teetotaler, it was unlikely that he would drink up his tips and the bar owner's profits.

What he did was to increase traffic and his popularity as a bartender. Along with dispensing booze at the bar, he served up a brand of humor that kept customers in stitches with laughter. On nights when the regular stand-up comedian failed to show up for his gig, the manager of the bar would ask Cosby to perform. He pocketed $25 for each gig. It didn't take long before his comedy capers were made known around town by word of mouth. With a little help from his cousin, Del Shields, then a popular radio disc jockey in Philly, the student-comedian was offered a job at The Cellar Club next door for $12.50 nightly.

After Shields showed him how to get more local booking, Cosby started taking his jokes seriously. He began taking notice of successful comedians and the materials they were using to get laughs. He borrowed from the more successful ones at that time—Dick Gregory, Bob Newhart, Nipsey Russell, Flip Wilson and Jonathan Winters. He wouldn't touch Redd Foxx's stuff.

With the arrival of 1962, Cosby began a series of departures from Temple to work weekends in New York City, where he got his first gig at the Gaslight Cafe in Greenwich Village. His pay check was $60, but by the time summer rolled around, the club paid him $175 weekly. It was at the Gaslight club that he began getting the attention of newspaper critics who reviewed his performances.

This led to a $200-a-week gig in Chicago at the Gate of Horn and the success of that stint led to a crisis in his educational pursuits at Temple. Now age 25, single and in possession of too much money to walk around with it in his pockets, Cosby found himself engaged in a wrestling match with his conscience. Should he remain at Temple for another two years and get his college degree or should he capitalize on his comedy talents?

It was not easy for him to decide whether he should take his mother's advice and get a college degree so he would have something to fall back on or whether he should keep being funny for money so he would have something to live on.

The decision was made more difficult by the fact that he was on an athletic tuition scholarship at Temple and would lose it if he didn't participate on the football and track teams. He was already burning the midnight oil trying to keep up with classroom work after team practices during the day and night club bookings at night.

By the end of 1962, he decided to drop out of Temple and go for the big bucks, promising himself to return in a few years after banking enough to pay his full tuition without relying upon an athletic scholarship.

With the dawn of 1963, the 26-year-old Cosby began crisscrossing the country with bookings at popular night clubs, including San Francisco's Hungry I, where Gregory was among the club's favorite drawing cards. By

*When he was not on the road performing or at a studio filming TV shows, Bill Cosby enjoyed spending time at home with his children playing games and watching TV.*

now, Cosby had decided against doing the topical racial jokes that Gregory had gained fame doing.

He told a reporter, "Some people call me the Philadelphia Dick Gregory, but that's silly...I found to be a success, I'd have to jump over Dick Gregory. I had to shadow Gregory in everything I did...I love Dick and we're good friends. But there's no comparison between us...I'm just a comedian who happens to be a Negro. I don't have the

*He was just plain Bill Cosby when on the TV location of I Spy in 1966. As he continued to create and his talents evolved with his academic discipline, the entertainer/educator has become Dr. William H. Cosby Jr., Doctor of Education.*

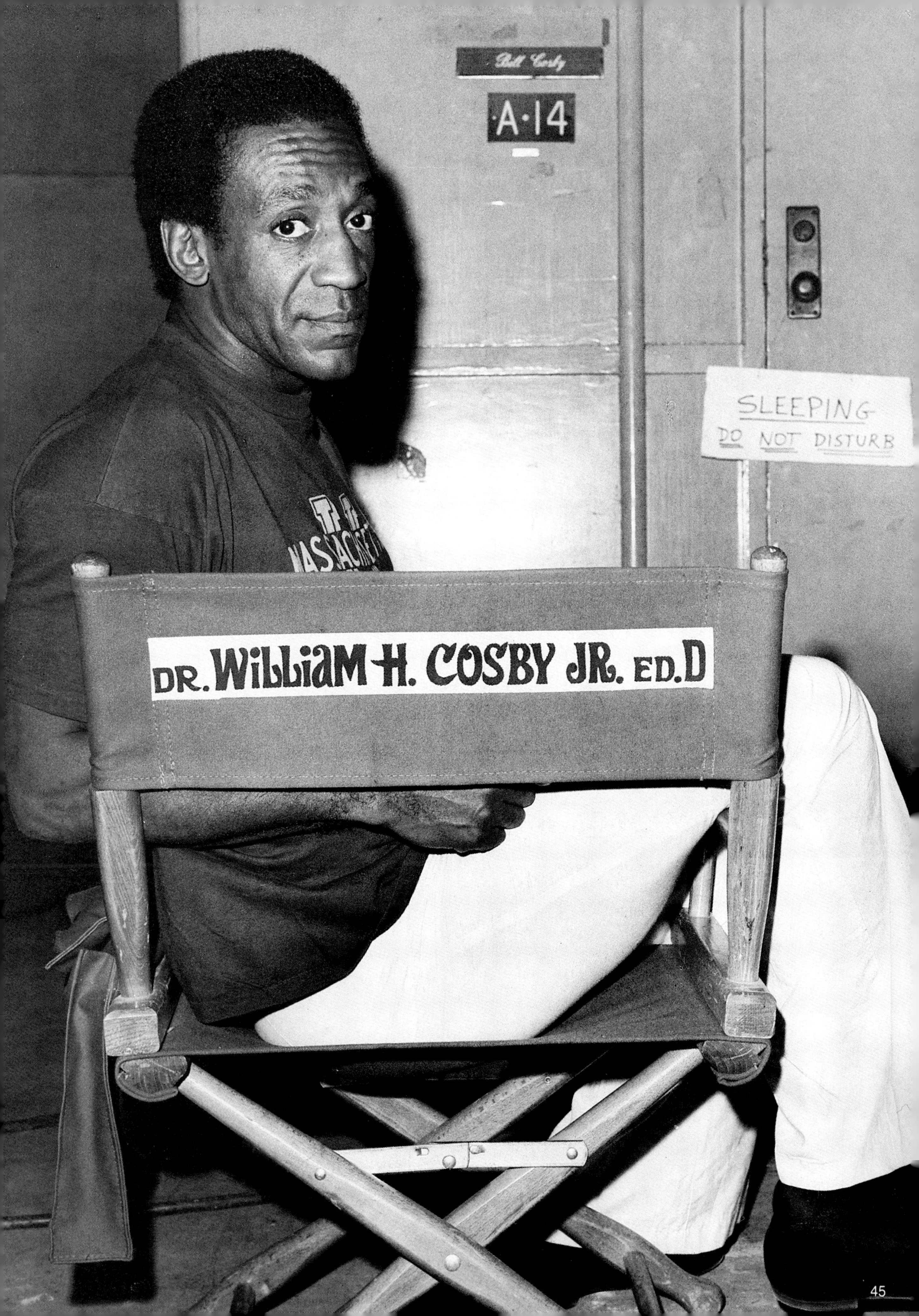
Bill Cosby
A·14
SLEEPING
DO NOT DISTURB
DR. WILLIAM H. COSBY JR. ED.D

guts to do what Dick does, either on the floor or off it."

He changed his routine to get away from some of the early material he had lifted from other comedians. He was succeeding in such a manner that he could then profess indifference to whether his material was being stolen by other comedians. Much later in his career he commented on this by saying, "If anyone else can get laughs with my stuff, they're welcome to it."

Cosby was on a roll. The bookings were coming in from all across the nation and that's when he decided that he needed a manager equal to his success.

*When* The Bill Cosby Show *began airing on TV in 1969, Cosby was cast in the role of a schoolteacher, a role he had aspired to play in real life. He chats with Elvira "Baby" Sanchez, mother of Sammy Davis Jr.*

The stage was set for the entrance of Roy Silver, who had successfully managed the career of Bob Dylan, and was launching his own company to manage entertainment talent. He promptly began lining up better club dates and helped Cosby land a recording contract with Warner Brothers to do comedy albums. During an appearance at the Bitter End club in 1963, Warner recorded live Cosby's first album. The title was *Bill Cosby Is A Very Funny Fellow...Right!* It was produced by Silver and Allan Sherman. In 1964, Warner released his second album called *I Started Out As A Child.*

*Cosby picked former Chicago disc jockey Sid McCoy to play a school principal in* The Bill Cosby Show.

*Singer/dancer Lola Falana made guest appearances as a performer on Cosby's TV shows.*

The album got more than $1 million in sales and a Grammy Award for Best Comedy Album of the Year.

That year, he started receiving top TV bookings and his career started zooming. His TV turning point came when he appeared as guest on Johnny Carson's *The Tonight Show* hosted by Allan Sherman, who co-produced his first album. TV Producer Sheldon Leonard, who had come up with an idea for a new action adventure series, saw Cosby's performance on the show and pegged him as a possibility to team with actor Robert Culp.

In 1976, Cos, a TV variety show, was canned because it didn't appeal to enough viewers to tune in for Bill Cosby. He had more success with his Fat Albert television show.

*In a scene from* The Cosby Show, *singer/actress Lena Horne made a guest appearance. In the episode, Dr. Cliff Huxtable was celebrating his birthday. The actor and Gloria Foster were co-stars of* To All My Friends On Shore, *which aired on TV in 1972.*

49

When NBC gave Leonard the go ahead with the project series called *I Spy*, he screen tested Cosby, who got the role.

With his signing on in the *I Spy* series, Cosby's career took a turn that would one day lead him to wearing the title as the most popular male performer on TV with a television show which he created: *The Cosby Show.*

While the year 1964 was a turning point in his show business career. That same year marked a turning point in his personal life. On January 25, 1964, Cosby married Camille Hanks, a shy and beautiful coed who was studying psychology at the University of Maryland when she met him on a blind date through mutual friends.

"I wasn't interested in having a blind date," Camille told EBONY Magazine, "especially with an entertainer. I thought of all the stereotypes, I suppose." They dated for the first time at a night club where Cosby was appearing. "I thought he was a very funny man," she recalls. "Afterwards, he sat in the car and talked all about himself, what he wanted to do about his future and everything. He had a great personality and was a lot of fun and I liked being out with him. He impressed me with his sincerity and humor."

The next weekend when he took her out again, he asked her to marry him. "I was quite shocked," she remembers. "We hadn't known each other long at all." She tried to make that point to him. But when he went back to New York, where he was performing, he phoned her every day. Smitten by her subtle sensuality and her cerebral conversations, Cosby stepped up his campaign by returning to the campus on weekends and taking her to the movies—where he often dozed off in a sound sleep. "That's when I fell in love with him," Camille says.

When school was recessed for the summer, Camille went to New York to visit relatives and adjusted their courtship to his busy schedule. By this time, her parents had peeped through her visits with relatives, and Cosby had seen through her true feelings for him. When he popped the question again, she said yes even though she knew her parents would object. Her father Guy Hanks, a Walter Reed General Hospital chemist, and her mother who operated a nursery didn't mask their feelings about the engagement. "They hadn't realized it had been that serious," Camille recalls. "The main thing my father objected to was my discontinuing school. My mother acted just like a mother. She just didn't want me to get married. I was only 19 and Bill was 26. Besides, they had stereotyped ideas about entertainers, too, and they just didn't like the idea of my being whisked away like that."

Since her parents hadn't made much progress trying to "talk some sense into her head," they had her leave New York and go spend the rest of the summer to

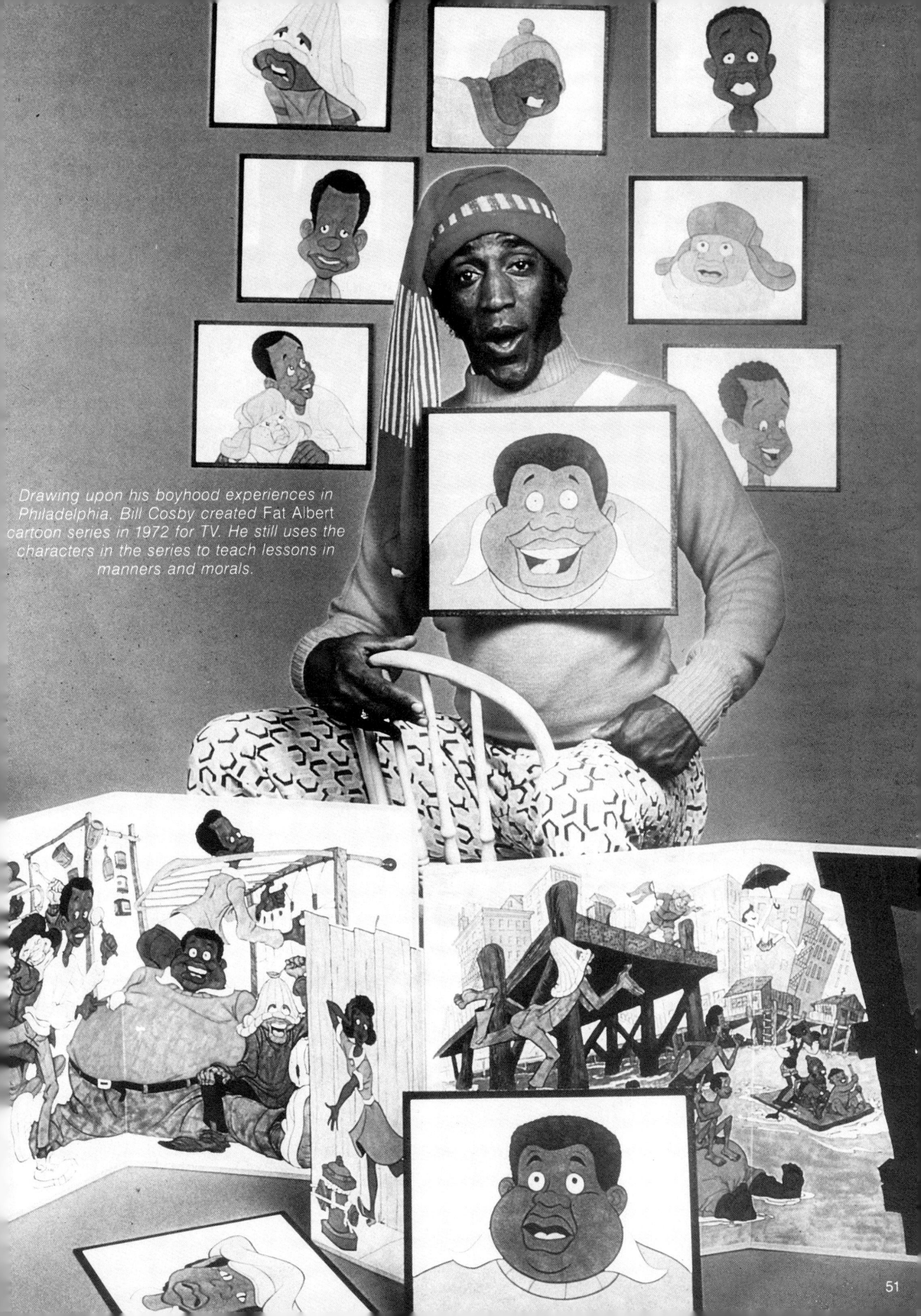

*Drawing upon his boyhood experiences in Philadelphia, Bill Cosby created Fat Albert cartoon series in 1972 for TV. He still uses the characters in the series to teach lessons in manners and morals.*

*Appearing before overflow crowd in 1970 at SCLC-Operation Breadbasket meeting in Chicago, Bill Cosby pledged support of the organization left as a legacy to Dr. Martin Luther King Jr., it's founder who was assassinated in Memphis, Tenn. on April 4, 1968.*

think things over with relatives in Virginia, the homestate of Cosby's parents. While there, she did have some second thoughts and decided to break off the engagement. She told EBONY that when she returned to school that fall, Cosby came back to Washington for a night club stint and called her. "I went out with him and I knew I wanted to marry him," she said in the interview. Cosby decided to approach the matter the old fashioned way. He went to her father and talked him into reluctantly letting go. However, her mother was never won over but did relax her stance enough to help with the wedding that took place in Olney, Md., on January 25, 1964.

Thus, life with Camille began. The first adjustment she had to make was to get used to being left to spend the night alone. She tried to get around this by going with him on club dates. This turned out to be tiresome. She was not accustomed to keeping such late hours. Nor was she used to meeting a lot of people. She explains: "I lost the privacy I had known all my life. I also had to get used to entertaining and smiling and being gracious. This is natural with Bill. He's much more of an extrovert than I am. He just loves people, period."

Cosby and Robert Culp, co-star in I Spy, applauded SCLC program presented by Rev. Jesse Jackson, head of Breadbasket. On one of many visits weekly from Los Angeles to Chicago, Cosby pledged continued support to Rev. Jackson. That support continued when Jackson later founded PUSH.

While she was slowly making adjustments to accommodate her husband's show biz lifestyle, Cosby's career made a sudden turn with a break on TV. When he won the co-starring role on *I Spy* with Robert Culp, that meant their home life would have more order and predictability. "Our life is altogether different with the television series," Camille gushed. "Bill works from eight until seven, usually, and he's home on weekends." When he travels abroad shooting, she accompanies him. By the time the second season rolled around, she could say, "When he travels abroad, we go

*Melting dad's heart during her moment on the center stage of his life, effervescent Ensa holds his hand and matches his tender smile. With brains and beauty under mortarboard, a radiant Mrs. Camille Cosby receives her master's degree in 1981 from the University of Massachusetts, where her husband earned both master's and doctorate degrees.*

with him," because their first child, Erika, was born. They traveled to Hong Kong, Japan, Mexico and Italy, she recalls.

With his $2,000-a-week income beginning with the 1965 debut of the series, Cosby leased an 11-room house, complete with swimming pool, in the prestigious Benedict Canyon community in Los Angeles.

She told EBONY what normal life was like for them. Although it meant that she would have him home in the evenings, it also meant sharing him with other people in his life. "He likes to have a lot of people in the house on his

*Relaxing in his Beverly Hills home, Bill Cosby watches TV with daughters (left) Erika and Erinn. As an advocate of selective viewing of TV programs for children, Cosby sets the example with his daughters. He still monitors programs for viewing in his home.*

*Proud parents Camille and Bill Cosby host a birthday party for daughter, Erinn, who was celebrating the 11th anniversary of her birth. Ensa sits at table with sister as they await the cutting of the cake. Neighborhood friends were among the invited guests.*

day off," she notes. "If we do go out, we must go to four or five places in one night." When he was not on the set before the camera, he is "tempermental," "impulsive," and "moody," she said and hastened to add: "He's a very considerate person. If he's going to be late, he always calls. He's very thoughtful: He remembers birthdays and anniversaries. He's a great father. He loves children and he's always a very good family man to his mother and his brothers."

She says he buys most of her clothes "because he likes to." He hardly leaves anything for her to do except stay charming and do the cooking. She usually prepares him "soul food" although, she says, he eats anything.

One plus in his having a co-starring role in the TV series is that he didn't have to do night club dates. Another was that he didn't have to try out new comedy routines on her. "In the beginning he did," she recalls, "but when you're intimate with someone, it's hard to see them as funny."

The first season of *I Spy* turned out to be a vintage year for Cosby. He copped the coveted Emmy Award as best actor in a dramatic series in 1966. The Emmy was a blessing because it gave him some leverage in his toe-to-toe slugfest to determine whether Cosby's character Alexander Scott will continue to be portrayed as an athletic-intellectual-flag-lover—who can only be linked with one female—his mother—or "all man," capable of kissing, hugging, talking softly.

Cosby had objected to his character being portrayed as a "jovial, good-natured celibate." He once told a newspaper columnist: "We travel to countries in Latin America, the Orient and Europe; I could get a girl any place. I don't care what she is."

After several months of good-natured negotiations, producer Sheldon Leonard caved in. Singer Nancy Wilson, whose ambition was to be an actress, was paired as the romantic interest of Cosby in her first network TV appearance in a dramatic role. Cosby was pleased with the choice and told JET: "She's a professional, more professional than I am."

For the next two years, 1967 and 1968, Cosby not only pioneered as the first Black actor in a co-starring role with a White actor, but he won Emmy awards for three consecutive years (1966-68) for Outstanding Performance by an Actor in a Leading Role in a Dramatic Series, *I Spy*.

During those three years, Cosby released three Warner Brothers albums: *Wonderfulness,* 1966; *Revenge,* 1967; and *To Russell My Brother Whom I Slept With,* 1968. Each LP won a Grammy Award for Best Comedy LP.

When the *I Spy* series ended after the 1968 season, Cosby was kept in the network stable and in 1969 returned to TV with NBC's "The Bill Cosby Special," a variety show. In 1970 "The

*Cosby plays role of Pronto, who accompanies Flip Wilson in role of The Lone Stranger. Riding their trusty steeds, the comedians appeared in a scene in 1973 on The Flip Wilson Show on NBC-TV.*

*When he hosted the Bell System Family Theatre special, "Highlights of Ringling Bros. and Barnum & Bailey Circus," in 1979, Cosby took his family with him. Camille holds baby Ensa, who applauds along with Erika (behind her mother), Cosby, Erinn and Ennis, who is obscured by Cosby's head.*

61

Second Bill Cosby Special" was aired on NBC. He returned the same year with a new series, *The Bill Cosby Show,* and was nominated for an Emmy, but lost to Room 222, which co-starred actress Denise Nicholas and actor Lloyd Haynes.

Nine years after he had dropped out of Temple University, vowing to return in 10 years to complete the two years left to earn a degree, Cosby made the decision to enroll again at Temple. He not only hung in until he received a B.A. degree from Temple, but entered an academic program at the University of Massachusetts that was flexible enough to allow him to earn a master's degree and a doctorate degree in education.

When he returned to Temple in 1971, he had time to get involved in another television series, *The Electric Company,* produced by PBS. He was associated with the series until 1976.

In another TV project, Cosby premiered on CBS a series called *Fat Albert and the Cosby Kids* in 1972. The success of Fat Albert led Cosby to include work on the show as part of his doctorate dissertation. He got approval from the University of Massachusetts and settled upon a title: *An Integration of The Visual Media Via Fat Albert And The Cosby Kids Into The Elementary School Curriculum As A Teaching Aid And Vehicle To Achieve Increased Learning.*

Before Cosby decided to teach manners and moral lessons on TV via Fat Albert, Saturday morning television had been snap, crackle and popping along its mindless, merry way.

"The show offers any parent or teacher an aid to discuss and to study mores and morals of society in a context where a child can learn," the comedian/actor/educator says. "It is not violent." The characters, modeled by Cosby's childhood buddies included: Dumb Donald, Weird Harold and Mushmouth. There was some concern expressed over the characterizations, Mushmouth, in particular. Cosby and Executive Producer Lou Scheimer wondered if children might feel the character was poking fun at speech impediments. "Instead," Schemimer allowed, "we were able to show kids that if you're different it doesn't mean you have no worth and can't have a good time."

To keep the show's authenticity, it varied topical issues. A special ad hoc advisory panel of academicians was formed by UCLA Graduate School of Education Associate Professor Gordon Berry, at Scheimer's urging. The Black professor assembled an impressive amalgam of child psychologists, psychiatrists and pysicists who haggled over scripts as if their very careers depended on it.

"I recall one meeting where we were arguing with a physicist from Oxford about cavemen as if we all knew one," Berry remembered in a JET interview.

*Comedian Bill Cosby is congratulated by Chancellor Randolph W. Bromery during graduation exercises at the University of Massachusetts, where the comedian became Dr. William H. Cosby Jr. with doctorate degree in education.*

"Another time I checked with a hospital to see if Fat Albert should be allowed to eat all the ice cream he wanted after his tonsils were removed. I talked to a psychologist, a pediatrician and finally a throat specialist, who said we could say he could eat ice cream but not all that he wanted."

Avidly interested in the effects of TV on social behavior, Berry says he got involved with *Fat Albert* "to introduce pro-social messages; provide ideas for writers and to look at such phenomena as death and its impact on children." A survey of 600 youngsters in five U.S. cities in the first year indicated that the carefully tailored Fat Albert messages got through. More than 85 percent of the respondents indicated that they could understand at least one message from a particular episode. These results pleased Cosby and the University of Massachusetts.

*Cosby appears at a 1969 benefit performance with Hollywood stars (left to right) Dean Martin, Burt Lancaster and Frank Sinatra.*

*During a 1967 trip to the Bahamas, Cosby visited home of actor Sidney Poitier along with Harry Belafonte. It was this occasion that the trio discussed making movies together that later resulted in film successes.*

66

*In a robbery scene from the film, Uptown Saturday Night, Cosby surrenders his money to hooded bandit. Actress Paula Kelly and actor Sidney Poitier are also hold-up victims. In inset photo, Cosby delivers a dramatic performance in a scene with famed dancer Harold Nicholas, who achieved fame with his brother, Fayard, as the dancing Nicholas Brothers.*

*As their romance blossoms in the 1977 movie,* A Piece Of The Action, *Bill Cosby and Denise Nicholas exchange an after dinner kiss.*

*Relaxing on location during the filming of* A Piece Of The Action, *Cosby poses with co-stars (l-r) Denise Nicholas, Tracy Reed and Hope Clarke.*

*A dramatic scene in the movie,* Uptown Saturday Night, *brings together the film's co-stars (l-r) Cosby, Sidney Poitier, Harry Belafonte and Calvin Lockhart.*

*As Barney Satin, the devil's assistant, Cosby gets startled reaction from Elliott Gould in* The Devil and Max Devlin. *Cosby grew a beard for the film,* Let's Do It Again, *which co-starred actor Sidney Poitier. Poitier also directed the comedy movie.*

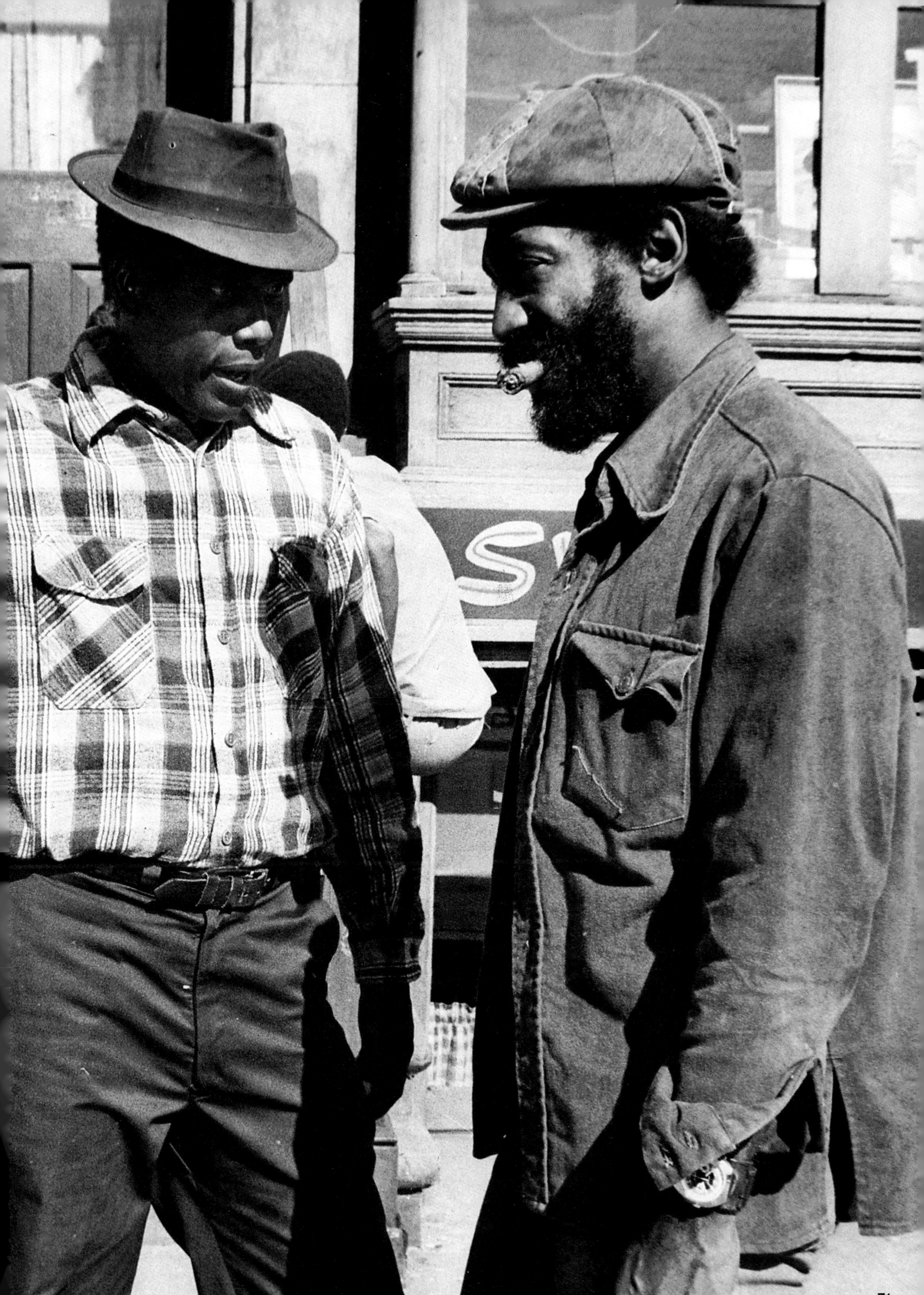

*Always willing to use his talent and money to support Blacks seeking elective offices, Cosby traveled to Gary, Ind., to support Mayor Richard Hatcher in the 1960s. He also supported Mayor Harold Washington of Chicago (right) and Mayor Marion Barry (below) of Washington, D.C.*

In May, 1977, the university conferred upon Cosby the Doctor of Education (E.D.D.) degree before a capacity commencement audience, including his mother Anna.

Cosby told JET that his mother was the happiest person at the graduation exercise. "She said to me, 'You finally got something that you can fall back on.' Cosby said that she apparently puts more trust in his education than his show biz talents that had already made him a multimillionaire.

The years 1971 to 1977 were not exclusively occupied with education projects via television.

At this point in his career that had earned him nearly $10 million, seven Grammy Awards for recordings and three Emmys as the best actor in a leading role in a dramatic series, the one thing Cosby had not done was make a movie.

The idea did not go away when he was told that major Hollywood studios were not interested in bankrolling his first film, *Man And Boy*. In fact, the idea gained impetus when his wife Camille cast the deciding vote for making the motion picture at their Jemmin, Inc., board meeting. "If you believe enough in the picture," she told him late one evening at home, "why don't you go ahead and put the money in it?" Cosby phoned Marvin Miller, who grew up in Cosby's Philadelphia neighborhood and produced Cosby's first NBC-TV series, to start moving with plans to make the movie.

*In Los Angeles, Cosby supported Mayor Tom Bradley in each bid to become the city's chief executive and gave money and support in his unsuccessful attempt to become the first Black governor of California. Mayor and Mrs. Bradley along with NAACP's Willis Edwards were on hand to honor Cosby as recipient of the Medgar Evers Award.*

*During summer of 1970, Bill Cosby helped Wilberforce University Alumni Association raise money to grant scholarships to Los Angeles students (left to right) Derrick Bell, Jefferson High; Labertha Maxwell, Jefferson High; Edna Anderson, Manuel Arts High and Odell Love, Freemont High. On a visit to Newark, N.J., Cosby confers with Ken Gibson, who became the city's first Black mayor.*

*Man And Boy* is a family western, in which his friend, actress Gloria Foster, is his leading lady and George Spell is cast as his son. It also stars actors Yaphet Kotto and Douglas Turner Ward. The film was special to Cosby because he put up $350,000 of his own money to make the movie when he couldn't interest a Hollywood filmmaker to produce it. "They just didn't want to see that many Black people in a cowboy picture," Cosby told EBONY in its April, 1971, issue. "The kind of reasons given are why Black actors don't act, Black directors don't direct and Black writers don't write as far as the screen is concerned," Cosby asserts. Produced by Cosby's production company, Jemmin, Inc., *Man And Boy* was made with a crew of 40 and a cast of 25 actors plus extras from Scottsdale, Arizona, where the film was made.

Cosby told EBONY in the April, 1971 cover story, "Friends, with tears in their eyes, said, 'If you don't get a studio to put up the money, don't make the picture.'" But Cosby said he was too much committed to the idea to heed what normally would have seem considered rock-sound advice.

The Jemmin production company caught Cosby's spirit, tackled the project and finished the film one week ahead of schedule.

On Easter of that year, movie audiences saw a premiere of *Man And Boy,* a two-hour film, described by Jemmin, Inc., as "a thinking man's

*A fan of trumpeter Miles Davis, Cosby observes at a 1983 ceremony when Davis donned an academic robe to receive an honorary doctorate degree from Fisk University President Walter Leonard. The trumpeter's wife actress Cicely Tyson, adjusts the hood on husband's gown.*

Western...basically; a truly moving and honest story of a Black family's struggle to exist in the troubled West after the Civil War."

In his next movie venture that year, Cosby was reunited with Robert Culp, co-star of the *I Spy* series, in a film called *Hickey and Boggs.* Culp also directed the detective movie in which actress Rosalind Cash had a starring role.

Two years later, in 1974, Cosby was back on a film location to co-star with Oscar-winning actor Sidney Poitier in a movie called *Uptown Saturday Night,* featuring the largest Black all-star cast in motion picture history.

Cast in *Uptown* with Poitier and Cosby were singer/actor Harry Belafonte, dancer Paula Kelly, comedians Flip Wilson and Richard Pryor, actress Rosalind Cash, actors

76

*During rehearsal for the NBC-TV Tonight Show which he served as guest host for Johnny Carson in 1970, Cosby keeps a straight face after telling a joke that evoked laughter from pianist Ahmad Jamal and singer Johnny "K" (right) in New York City.*

*Plucking the bass violin, Cosby sometimes performs with musical groups booked on shows that he headlines as a comedian. He prefers jazz music and boosts the Black musicians who struggle to keep alive the art form.*

*Cosby chats with two lovely ladies, Natalie Cole and Phyllis Hyman (right), as the two singers dine together. Famous fashion model Iman embraces Cosby on set of* The Cosby Show *during 1985 season.*

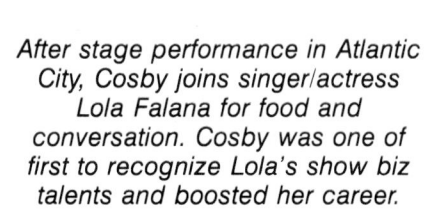

*After stage performance in Atlantic City, Cosby joins singer/actress Lola Falana for food and conversation. Cosby was one of first to recognize Lola's show biz talents and boosted her career.*

Cosby always used his influence to help careers of entertainers like actress Beah Richards (left) and singer/actress Patti LaBelle, who lives in Philadelphia.

*Cosby joins (left to right) pianist Skitch Henderson, actor Lorne Greene, and actor Robert Culp onstage in Chicago at 1966 National Association for Broadcasters convention.*

Roscoe Lee Browne, Calvin Lockhart, Johnny Sekka and Lincoln Kilpatrick.

While visiting Nassau, Bahamas, where Poitier has a home, Cosby was asked by the Academy winner to be his co-star. Cosby looked over the script, agreed and when he saw the finished product, he was delighted. Cosby, during an interview for a JET cover story (June 25, 1974), that featured him and Poitier, was enthusiastic. "This movie probably is the first first-class comedy that Black people will be able to see," Cosby says. "It's clean; the material is clean, no foul language whatsoever. You can take anybody from your seven-year-old to your 87-year-old to see it, and they're gonna have a ball," he adds.

*Uptown Saturday Night* became a smash box office hit. During its first week's run in New York, Detroit and Chicago, the film ranked No. 6 on Variety trade publication's "50 Top-Grossing Films" chart, trailing only behind such long-running award winners as *Exorcist* and *Sting*.

Warner Brothers, which distributed the film, says it pulled in $9 million in domestic rentals.

Anticipating the jingle of cash registers at theater box offices again, Cosby teamed with Poitier in 1975 to film, *Let's Do It Again.* They headlined a brilliant cast of stars that included actresses Denise Nicholas, Lee Chamberlain and Jayne Kennedy; actors Calvin Lockhart, John Amos,

*Cosby considers actress Janet MacLachlan as one of best leading ladies cast in films with him.*

Cosby used Fat Albert TV show get across the message that voteless people is a hopeles people." He has helped raise political funds for Blacks seek elective offices in many cities a states.

Ossie Davis, Jimmie Walker and singer Billy Eckstine.

The film, with its all-star cast, was another hit. It grossed $15 million and won critical acclaim. JET's cover story (November 13, 1975), said that *Let's Do It Again* is "unique in presenting Blacks in historically true situations, something rarely seen on American movie screens..."

Obviously smitten by the accolades showered upon him for his roles on the big screen, Cosby returned to a Hollywood movie set to film *Mother, Jugs And Speed* in 1976. The cast included Raquel Welch, Larry Hagman, Dick Butkus, Valerie Curtin, Bill Henderson and Harvey Keitel.

A year later, in 1977, Cosby was teamed for the third time with Sidney Poitier as co-stars of *A Piece Of The Action.* Like *Uptown Saturday Night* and *Let's Do It Again,* Cosby and Poitier were supported by a scintillating cast of Black actors and actresses, including James Earl Jones, Denise Nicholas, Tracy Reed, Hope Clark and Sheryl Lee Ralph.

In a cover story (October, 27, 1977), which features the film's co-starring couples, Cosby and Denise Nicholas and Poitier and Tracy Reed, JET says the film deals honestly with some social problems that open deep wounds. The newsmagazine notes, however, that director Poitier "coats them (wounds) and laces them with the type of chemically balanced situation comedy

*A role model for children of all colors and creeds, Cosby is concerned that they learn to cope without a clash of colors and cultures. After playing tennis to support a charity, he rushed to New York's Town Hall to support concert recital by Newark Boys Chorus. He also gave boost to celebration of National Library Week.*

# READ

Bill Cosby
and Friends
for America's
Libraries

Following a "Save The Children" rally in San Francisco sponsored by Rev. Cecil Williams, pastor of Glide's church, Bill Cosby greets some children inside the pastor's study room. The Christmas celebration attracted a huge crowd, reflecting the San Francisco multi-racial society.

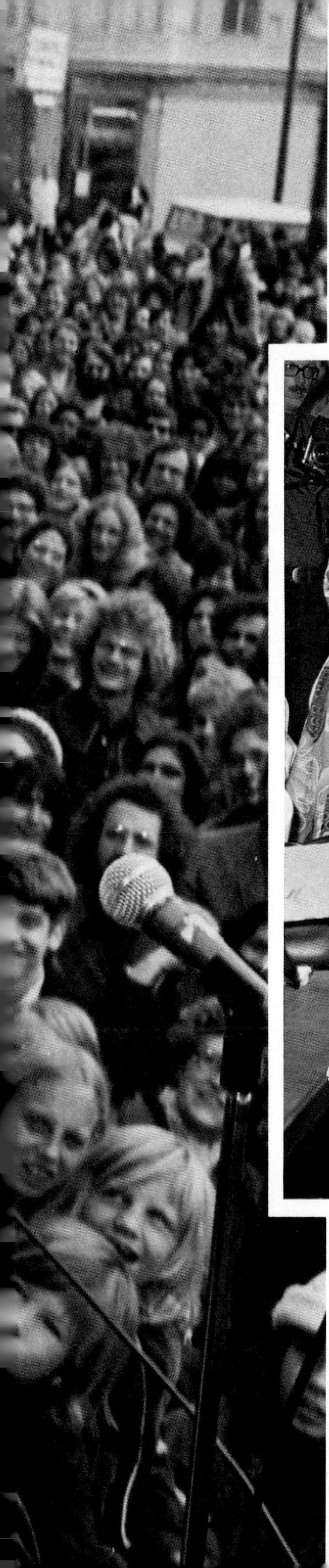
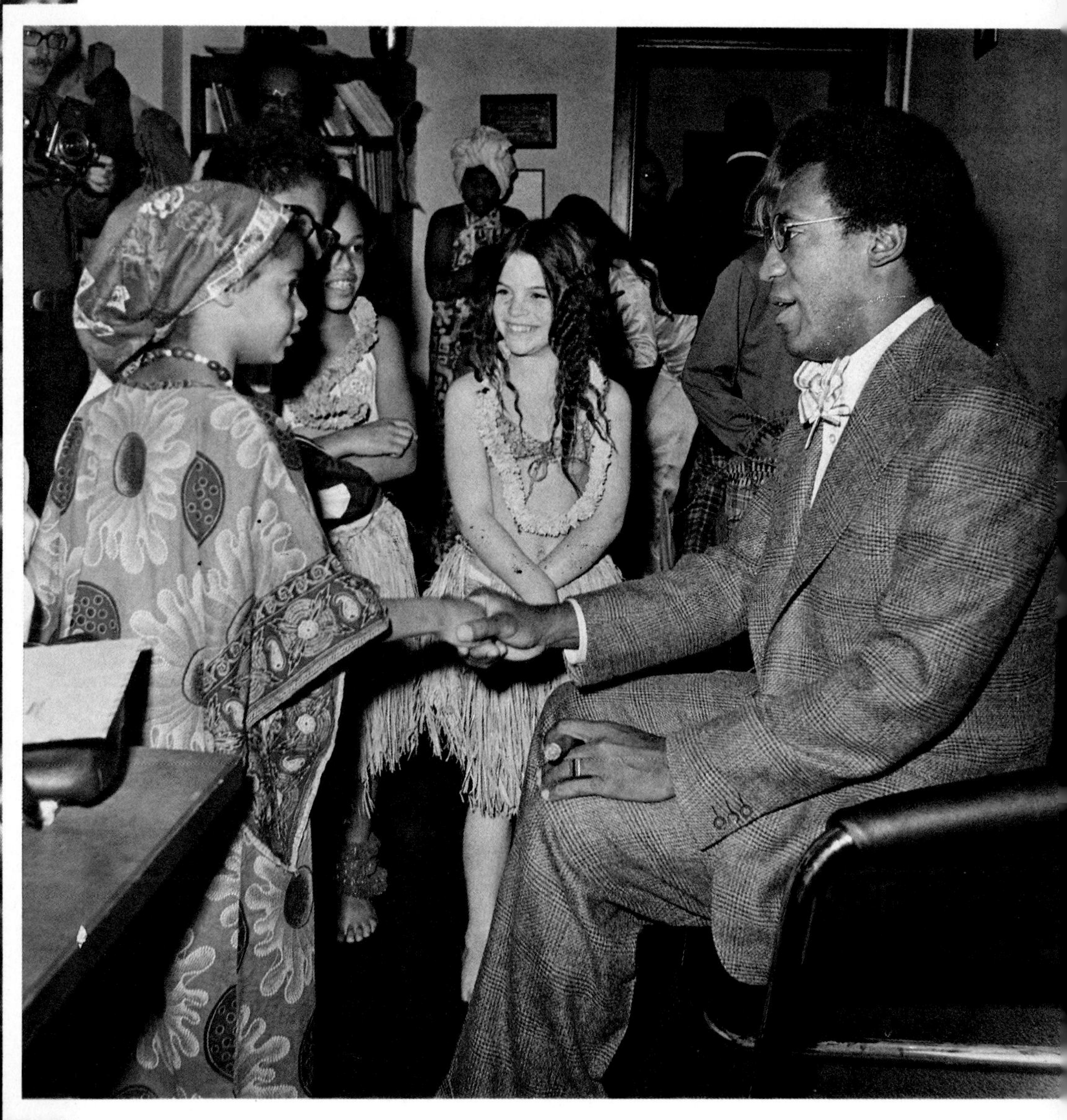

*Remembering the streets of Philadelphia, where he grew up, Bill Cosby finds it easy to relate to Black kids. He sometimes joins in games they play so he can gain their confidence and encourage them to develop good character and study habits.*

that only he and his trusty sidekick co-star Bill Cosby can muster...He (Poitier) has in this new $3 million film, touchingly combined Black hurt and Black humor, Black cunning with Black conscience."

Cosby, now an established box office attraction in theaters, continued his film presence in 1978 when he landed a starring role in *California Suite.* It was his first attempt at slapstick comedy and the cast includes Richard Pryor, Sheilah Frazier, Gloria Gifford, Alan Alda, Jane Fonda, Walter Matthau, Elaine May, Maggie Smith and Michael Caine.

His eighth motion picture was filmed in 1981. In the movie, *The Devil And Max Devlin,* Cosby plays the role of the devil and co-star Elliott Gould is cast as Max Devlin.

*The Devil And Max Devlin* was the last motion picture he made and the first one he did since another turning point occurred in his show biz career.

Cosby had been living a charmed life, having succeeded in night clubs, on concert stages, on comedy and musical albums, in television series and motion pictures. But he felt that he was drowning in his own success because he had control over his *show* but not his *business.*

He talked about this turnaround in an interview for a JET cover story (May 11, 1978). Cosby reveals that he had revamped his business team and shifted responsibilities. In the restructured set up, he said, "Camille and I are the only ones who sign our checks. I got rid of my manager. He took "X" and I took "Y". I retained the William Morris Agency (a talent representative), hired an accounting firm and three lawyers. I have no manager." He explains what happened:

"When that break (with his manager) occurred, I was on the decline as far as big rooms (in night clubs) were concerned. I was in a pinch. Before, in order to make $2 million, I worked five months. After the break, I had to go out and work all year to make that."

To put brakes on the downward skid, Cosby gave up the fast-lane living of Beverly Hills life for a small town in Massachusetts. He purchased a home for $65,000 and spent $300,000 renovating and redecorating the interior. He cut back on other expenses and lived off $750,000 a year, a sum that may cause eyes to pop everywhere except in Hollywood.

He installed Camille, who was completing her master's degree, as a bonafide vice president of his film and recording operations and before you could say Fat Albert, he was back to his five-month $2 million schedule. And because of the success of *Fat Albert And The Cosby Kids* cartoon series, Bill and Camille could remain millionaires if they did nothing more than count their money.

Camille's vice president stripes were both earned and conferred. After all, Cosby could just as well have kept Camille out of his business and weaned her on a fat weekly allowance. Some male stars, or working men, have trouble mixing daytime financial sheets and nighttime bed sheets with their wives. But Camille took her executive lumps right alongside Bill's career slumps.

In retracing the turnabout as he faced a financial crisis, Cosby recalls sitting in their 31-room Beverly Hills mansion where he had a small fleet of luxury cars.

"I looked at Camille and said we have to decide what we are going to do. First, I told her we have each other. Then I asked how important is all of this as I waved my hand across the interior of our Beverly Hills home. I asked her if we needed this stuff around. She told me to do what I wanted to do because she's my wife.

"As funny as it sounds, I asked her if she thought she could live off $750,000 a year—keep in mind the scale we were living on. She said 'yes' so I began cutting back. I said we'll get away from here (Los Angeles) and survive off what we do as a business."

Cosby conferred with business associates Atty. Charles Lloyd and accountant Ernest L. Aubrey about ending his one-third interest in the Campbell, Silver, Cosby Corp., and getting rid of his corporation co-partner, Roy Silver, as his personal manager. "We're trying to eliminate all dealings

*Although he never borrowed an X-rated joke from Redd Foxx, comedian Bill Cosby says the comic, whose Sanford And Son series was a success, belongs on TV again with another sitcom.*

*Taking advice from his book, Bill Cosby's Personal Guide To Tennis Power, Cosby says: "When you see the ball coming, don't pull your racquet back right away (even though you paid $8 to $20 a half-hour to have someone yell this at you). Have a little conversation with yourself: 'Gee, he hit it! It's coming at me! Oh God.'"*

# Teasing Tutor

In his 'I Spy' TV series, Bill Cosby was convincing as a tennis pro, but that was mediocre compared with his real life court play since then. After countless lessons from some of the best tennis teachers, he not only became one of the best players on the tennis celebrity circuit, he authored an illustrated book titled Bill Cosby's Personal Guide To Tennis Power. He dedicated the book to all of his pro instructors who, he said, were paid "to make Bill Cosby look a lot better than he really is while on the tennis court playing against other celebrities to try and win a trophy for his beautiful wife Camille, who is going to be very angry because he left home to have fun without her."

A frequent headliner at JET Celebrity Tennis Tournaments in the 1970s, Cosby often distracted his opponents by clowning and offering advice on how they should play the game.

In his tennis book, he suggests that a tennis ball could very well hold the key to a player's game. So he offers this advice: "Try to buy intelligent balls, ones that know what you mean to hit and not what you did hit. Those that go over the net—not into it. In purchasing your ball, remember that the more intelligent the ball is, the more sensitive it is. Actually, the ball is very insecure. It has a fantastic ego. If you do not look at it all of the time and give it all of your attention, it will not do what you want it to do. It will refuse to behave properly."

With wife Camille, Cosby awaits turn to play in a celebrity tennis tournament (above). With daughter, Erika, he sits in stands before playing in a JET Celebrity Tennis Tournament to benefit United Negro College Fund (UNCF).

*In 1971, Cosby was introduced at tennis tournament by former Wimbledon champ Arthur Ashe. Cosby once said he, "eats everything Arthur Ashe eats in the vain hope that one day I will be able to return one of his serves at which point I will run around the court trying to sell the racquet."*

Following a 1975 JET Celebrity Tennis Tournament sponsored by American Airlines in Los Angeles, Cosby poses with participants (l-r) actress Denise Nicholas, Dr. CLyde Freeman, Mrs. Oscar Robertson. Actress Gloria Foster, his co-star in Man And Boy, was a spectator.

At a 1976 Lauder's King of the Hill Pro Celebrity Tennis Tournament in New York City, Cosby greets Hiram Walker Co. President Roy W. Stevens. Actor Charlton Heston was doubles partner with Cosby.

Cosby, once the fifth-ranked celebrity tennis player in the world, has two avid supporters, actress Sheila Frazier and his wife Camille. At Louis Armstrong Stadium in New York City, Cosby and sportscaster Howard Cosell are video taped by former Wimbledon tennis champ Virginia Wade.

*During a break in the 1986 U.S. Open Tennis Tournament in New York City, Cosby visits with the world's best tennis player, Martina Navratilova and ABC-TV journalist Kathleen Sullivan.*

*Nursing a sprained ankle while playing tennis at a 1981 celebrity tournament he hosted in Atlantic City to benefit the United Negro College Fund, Cosby is comforted by Playboy Bunnies who were ushers at the tennis event.*

*In 1972, Cosby watched the antics of Meadowlark Lemon, captain of the Harlem Globetrotters basketball team which Cosby joined for an exhibition game.*

*Valerie Brisco-Hooks, three-time Olympic gold medalist, gives Cosby a friendly pat as she speeds past him during a race at Penn Relays which was taped for The Cosby Show. While dining out, Cosby catches upon the happenings reported in JET.*

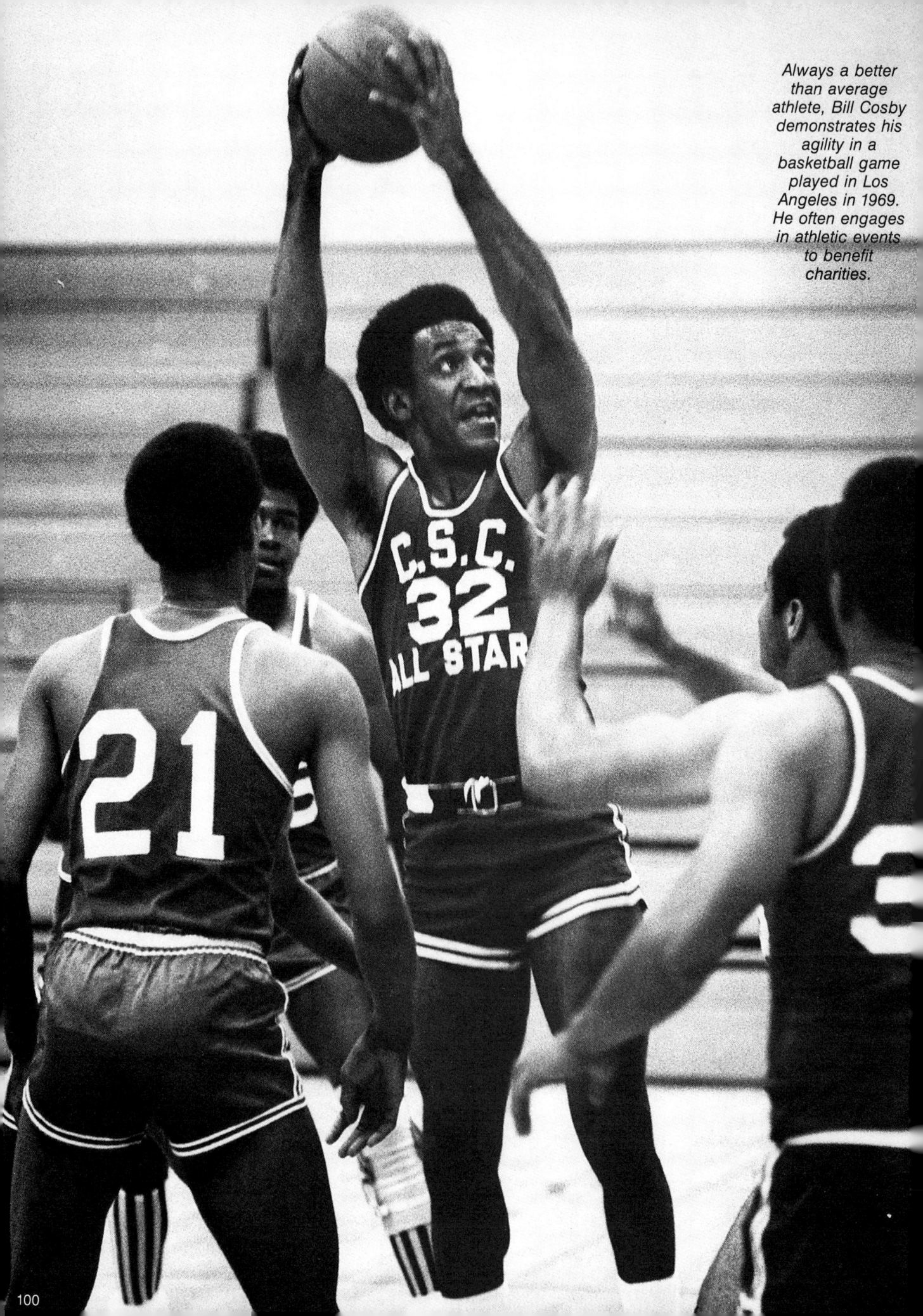

Always a better than average athlete, Bill Cosby demonstrates his agility in a basketball game played in Los Angeles in 1969. He often engages in athletic events to benefit charities.

*Before donning boxing gear in a Los Angeles gym with boxer Hedgemon Lewis in 1968, Cosby took out insurance by wearing eyeglasses. In 1970, Cosby worked out with the Toronto Argonauts of the Canadian Football League.*

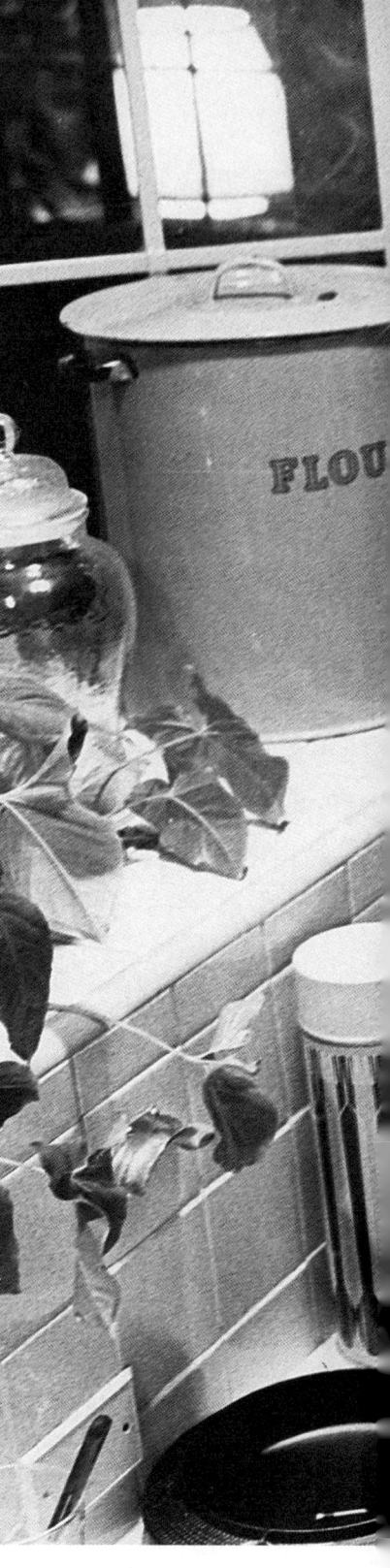

*Wearing T-shirt that says "Camille's Husband," Cosby spends quality time at home with son, Ennis William. In role of househusband Cosby relieves wife of kitchen chores.*

with Mr. Silver," Cosby states. Because Cosby was the primary money-maker of the Campbell, Silver, Cosby Corp., which had some $30 million worth of projects in the offing, the entertainer business man felt that the time had come for him to have a bigger cut of the money. Silver, in his position as co-partner of the corporation, was opposed to Cosby getting a larger piece of the action. This struck the comedy king as being funny—not affording light mirth and laughter—but funny that suggests suspicion. As his manager,

Silver should have been all for it, Cosby reasoned thus he saw the matter as a conflict of interest and fired Silver as his personal manager.

"I took on a male executive secretary and hired a secretary for him. Then I hired another man to take care of the cars in California and we moved to Petersham, Mass. I went to work on my master's (degree) and we lived off the gigs I picked up usually at $5,000 per night, or $10,000 if I was lucky."

In cutting expenses by cutting back on their Los Angeles lifestyle, the

Cosbys made a smooth move to Massachusetts. This prompted Camille to comment to JET: "Bill has learned to say 'no' and has matured businesswise, too." He returned the compliment, saying: "Camille's not just the mother of my children. She's really my partner. She's for real. She's paid a salary and she does whatever she wants with her money."

He says he is fortunate because his business is Camille's business and when he goes to bed at night he only has to look over his shoulder to see how the other half of the corporation is doing.

When Cosby shifted directions in 1971 from recordings and television to make movies, he did not abandon them. Along with his goal of adding movies to his list of show business credits, Cosby was even still determined to complete the education he had started at Temple University.

The sweet smell of success of his three years with the *I Spy* TV series—1965 to 1968—had turned sour by his failure to capitalize on his own NBC-TV show in 1969. He had won three Emmy's, one for each year of the *I Spy* series, and he had hoped his popularity would be transferred to his own series, *The Bill Cosby Show,* which premiered on NBC in September, 1969, and folded during the summer of 1971.

In this new series, Cosby played the role of Chester "Chet" Kincaid, a schoolteacher. The supporting cast included actress Lillian Randolph the first year and actress Beah Richards the following season. Singer/actress Olga James, who married celebrated alto saxophonist Cannonball Adderly (now deceased), was also a member of the cast along with Sid McCoy, who was a popular radio disc jockey in Chicago before he settled in Hollywood to become an actor and film director.

Everyone who knows Cosby also knows that his first aspiration was that of becoming a school teacher. He was living that daydream as Kincaid in the television series and was naturally disappointed when NBC dropped the show.

However, Cosby continued his quest for teaching on television when he turned up on *The Electric Company* for PBS, where he was a guest star along with such actresses as Rita Moreno, Lee Chamberlin and Irene Cara. He continued that association with the public broadcasting network until 1976.

In September 1972, Cosby made a two-pronged move on television, Having made an unsuccessful bid at NBC with *The Bill Cosby Show,* he took his talent and ideas to CBS. On September 9, he premiered *Fat Albert And The Cosby Kids,* starring himself in a subtle teaching role. The show was an instant hit. In the fall of 1979, the cartoon show changed its name to *The New Fat Albert Show.*

Two days after in introducing *Fat Albert And The Cosby Kids* to a CBS

At the 1979 JET Celebrity Tennis Tournament in Atlanta, Bill Cosby roasted popular politician Andrew Young. An avid tennis player, too, Young used sport to unwind as Ambassador to the United Nations and later as mayor of Atlanta.

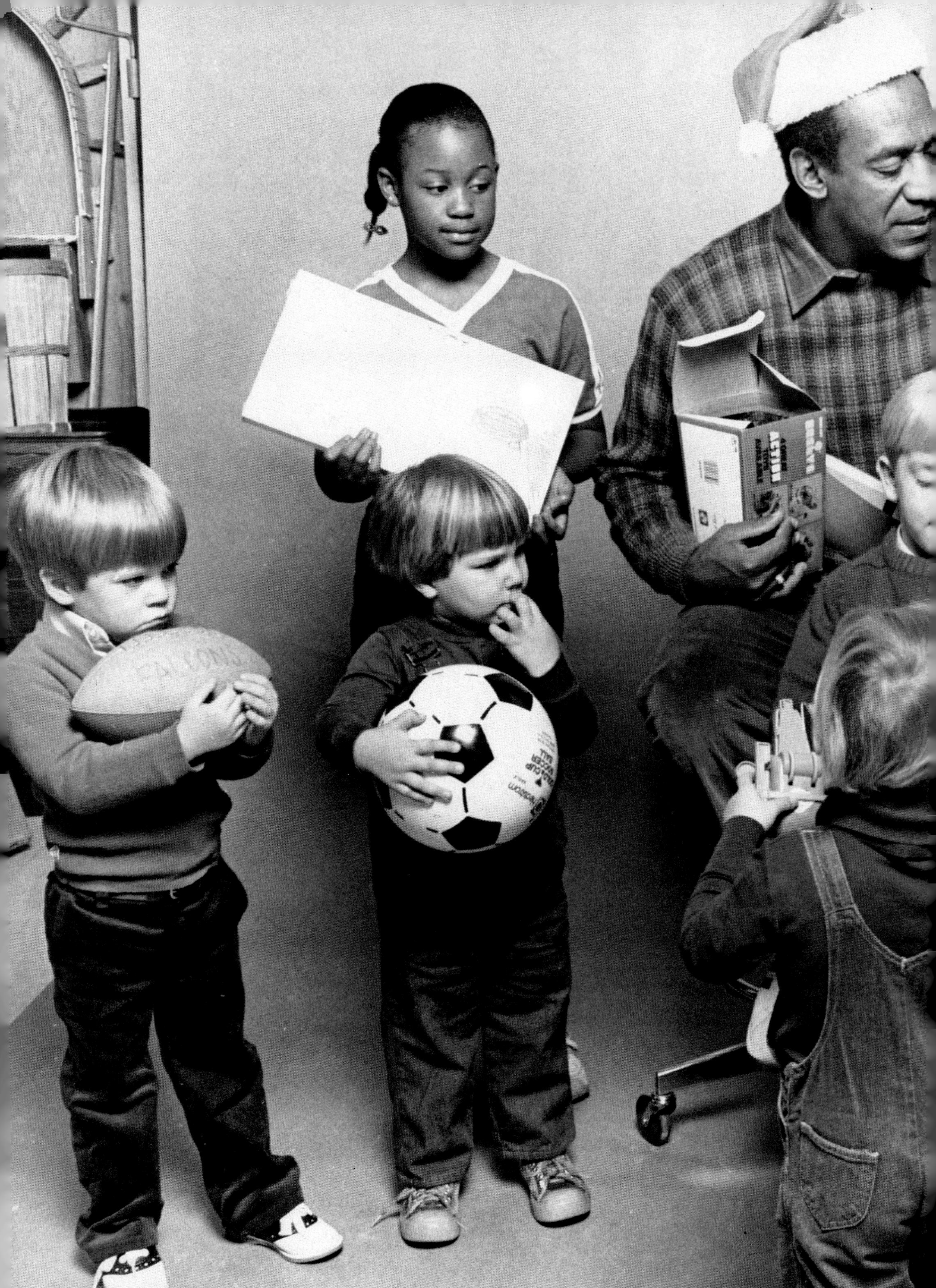

*Because of his friendship with Atlanta Mayor Andrew Young, the city's second Black chief executive, Bill Cosby took time out to play Santa Claus in 1983 for needy children. The toy drive made Christmas merry for cheerful children.*

audience, he premiered *The New Bill Cosby Show* on CBS. Appearing in the starring role, Cosby had a regular cast that included the sensational Donald McKayle Dancers, comedian Foster Brooks and Grammy Award-winning Quincy Jones, who conducted the orchestra. Eight months later, CBS canceled the show.

Three years later, on September 19, 1976, Cosby carried some television ideas for a new variety show to ABC. The show, titled *Cos,* was hosted by the comedian. Regulars on the show included Jeff Altman, Marion Ramsey, Charlie Callas and popular drummer

Willie Bobo, now deceased. The show was canceled the following month on October 31, 1976.

It was no consolation to Cosby when he was told that his three failures had nothing to do with his talents or ideas. The problem, some said, was created by the success of two other Black January 14, 1972, his show, *Sanford And Son,* frequently was No. 1 in the ratings and remained in the top 10 until its last telecast on September 2, 1977.

Cosby, who didn't return to television again until eight years later when he premiered *The Cosby Show* on September 20, 1984, a family situation

*A friend and supporter of the NAACP, Bill Cosby joins with entertainer Sammy Davis Jr. to perform at a 1984 benefit in Gary, Ind. After appearing as a special guest on program at Brooklyn College for the Ethiopian Relief Benefit, Cosby gets a kiss from Ann Bing, who participated in the fund raiser.*

comedians, Flip Wilson and Redd Foxx, whose shows were constantly in the top 10 rated by the Nielsen surveys. From 1970 to 1974, *The Flip Wilson Show* helped keep NBC in the ratings race among network competition from CBS and ABC. When Redd Foxx was added to NBC's situation comedy lineup on comedy that became an instant success, didn't accept the reason advanced for the demise of his three previous TV shows. He didn't buy the suggestions that the network brass couldn't tolerate having three Black comedians on the air with successful shows.

In a revealing interview with this writer at his home in New York City in April 1985, Cosby talked frankly about his failures in TV before his *The Cosby Show* lifted NBC to the top while the show also held the No. 1 rating in the 1984 season and the 1985 summer rerun season.

Seated on a sofa in the living room of his family's New York brownstone home, Cosby first expressed disappointment that Redd Foxx, at that time, did not have his own show. "One of the things that I don't understand is how they (network bosses) can exclude Redd Foxx. I don't accept the fact that someone has not pulled up to his house as of yet with a whole Brinks' truck full of money and said, 'Redd, please come back.'"

Cosby then leaned closer to the tape recorder and declared: "If Redd is not picked up, I'll go get Redd, because Redd knows how to do two things very well. One is be funny and the other thing is have a soft ear for any person with a sad story."

Recalling the fuss that was kicked up when Foxx, riding a crest of popularity and enjoying top ratings, requested a dressing room with a window, Cosby said: "The position that Redd was in, they should have knocked a wall out."

Cosby said that Foxx is a man of principles and should be returned as a star. "He cannot come back for less than when he left and you can't treat him like he is some neophyte," Cosby allowed. "With the track record that Redd has off *Sanford And Son,* if Bill Cosby was making X amount of money, then I'm afraid that they would have to pay Redd the same amount of money because Redd has already proven his worth," Cosby said and added with emphasis: "Cosby came in without a proven track record. The longest show I was on was three years. The next show was two years. Then after that it was 24 shows, and then it was 13 and then I was gone. I made a joke about it. I said, the next time I come on, I'll get a one-show guarantee or a half hour guarantee on a one-hour show. They will pick up the second half hour if it looks good."

Less than six weeks after Cosby expressed his views about Foxx, the veteran funny man was back on TV, starring in *The Redd Foxx Show* for ABC-TV. It was later canceled.

For nearly a decade (1976 to 1984) when he was not star of a television series, Cosby used that time to do a variety of things, including getting closer to wife Camille and their children (Erika Ranee, Erinn Chalene, Ensa Camille, Evin Harrah and Ennis William), playing tennis for charitable causes; supporting civil rights, political, educational and social organizations and institutions; making musical albums; performing regularly in top night clubs and collecting awards.

At the mere mentioning of Camille's name, Cosby will place his wife on a

*In 1985, Cosby came to the aid of Coretta Scott King, widow of Mobel Peace Prize winner Dr. Martin Luther King Jr., as headliner of the Partnership of Dreams, honoring the Martin Luther King Jr. Center for Non-Violent Social Change.*

*Bill Cosby hugs Mrs. Coretta Scott King as he joins with Chairman J.W. Marriott Jr. in Atlanta to salute the Martin Luther King Jr. Center. Mrs. King's son, Dexter, gives Cosby portrait of Dr. King for headlining tribute.*

pedestal of praise, emphasizing that she is the secret of his success and the reason more fame and fortune have come his way than he had ever hoped to see.

At every crossroad in his career, she was there to point him in the right direction, he says. A lot of people figure that the best way to get to him or influence him on a course of action would be through charming or coaxing Camille. Cosby says that doesn't work in his household. "People would rather deal with me than with Camille," he

*Mrs. King received support from EBONY/JET Publisher John H. Johnson and Coca Cola USA President Brian G. Dyson. Johnson and Cosby reflect upon the $300,000 which was raised at the "Partnership of Dreams" tribute dinner.*

confides. "She's rough to deal with when it comes to my business." He made that observation to JET in June of 1979 at his Los Angeles home as he handled household chores while wearing a T-shirt bearing the message: "Camille's husband."

He offers an insight into her discerning mind. When he went on European locations in the late '70s to shoot two made-for TV films, *Top Secret* and *Sitting Pretty,* Cosby offered her a job as a still photographer, paying $500 weekly and per diem (based on her service by the day).

"The woman got mad with me because I took her taxes out," he allowed. "When I paid her—this is my corporation and she's vice president— I told the accountant to take out her federal and state taxes, social security and whatever else. I think she wound up with maybe $300. Oh, she was mad!"

Noting that his wife cares about the images he has projected throughout his career, Cosby says he will never have to worry about being remembered the uncomplimentary ways some of America's Black heroes have been portrayed in so-called "life story" movies or TV docu-dramas.

"Should anyone do my life story, there will be no rushing Camille into approving a script that makes me look like an indecisive, eyeball-rolling, head-scratching, foot-shuffling Uncle Tom. She'd never approve that kind of

In 1982, Rev. Jesse Jackson presents a collector's painting to Bill Cosby and his wife Camille for their support of PUSH fund raiser in Chicago.

thing. I have faith in that," he brags.

Spending more time with his five young children during this period of his life was especially rewarding to Cosby. He talked of his relationship with their first-born child, Erika Ranee, then 12 years old, who was with him in Chicago, where he was performing in a night club. He said part of the reason for her being with him on the club date was "just hanging out with dad." The other part is this: "I show her box office receipts. I show her how to count money... These are things that have to do with the business." He elaborates:

"There are so many entertainers who don't know how a dollar is generated or where it goes or what was spent going in and what's owed going out... I don't ever want my children to feel that what I'm doing is magical. I'm not a magical person. I'm an artist and I want them to see me making my sketches and building so that they see the real thing. I just don't want them to think that I get up in the morning and go to the set and things just jump out of my head, because if that is what they think, then they are going to fail."

He feels that Erika, who is now enrolled in Wesleyan University in Middletown, Conn., will find that experience valuable in whatever career she chooses. Erika is no longer a source of material for some of his comedy routines like she was when Cosby was once asked, who are your favorite comedians? With a straight face, he answered: "My Daughter, Erika. She's the funniest person I know — got a C minus average in high school and says she wants to go to Yale."

Cosby found humor in the childish behavior of his other children — Erinn, Ennis, Ensa and Evin. Their cute and comic capers became part of his night club act and record albums. During this period in their lives, he has become so involved with helping them to mature that he doesn't find much that is funny in their behavior. Erinn, at 19, was a freshman at Spelman College for women in Atlanta and Ennis, in high school, may enter Morehouse College for men in the same city. Upon receiving an honorary doctorate degree (LL.D) from Morehouse in February 1986, Cosby phoned his son, Ennis, and told him about the college that had graduated Nobel Peace Prize winner Dr. Martin Luther King, Jr., and many other celebrated alumni.

"Son" he said jokingly, "I've struck a deal at this wonderful college. I have an agreement that you will be allowed to enroll at Morehouse as the first underachiever ever admitted."

This was a special proud moment for Cosby in the new relationship he had established with 17-year-old Ennis, who had once put undue stress upon him.

He talked about that in a JET cover story (May 30, 1983):

"As a celebrity, I've run into the same problems that many celebrities run into having children," Cosby allowed. "The

"Don't let Camille's smile fool you," Cosby says of his wife in role as a businesswoman. "She's tougher to deal with than I am," he adds. That explains why he oftens takes the back seat to her.

*At a benefit performance in Washington, D.C., Cosby was co-host with actress Debbie Allen, whose sister, Phylicia Rashad, stars on his show. Dizzy Gillespie was a performer.*

peers of the children jump on them. 'Oh, your father is a big person,' they say to them. They come home beaten up and they come home beaten down by their peers." The affect on his 14-year-old son was so harmful that the teenager "was combating education and winning." Cosby explains:

"Education was coming to the child and he was fighting it off. He said, 'I'm not studying nothing. You show me a book and I'll fall asleep. You want me to know English, forget it. I don't want to know from English. I don't want to know from anybody."

The boy's teacher reminded Cosby, who has earned a Ph.D. degree in education, of the high cost of the youth's schooling and asked, "Why does your kid owe us 12 years of homework?" That was when the youngster was 12 years old, Cosby recalls and remembers the excuse offered. "He said: 'I was robbed. I was on my way to school and this cat came with a gun and... took my homework, not money, not clothing, just wanted my homework.'"

That was a lie, Cosby learned, and the father didn't "spare the rod" for fear that he would "spoil the child." He became a good student after they had physical encounter.

He said he took his son to the barn to do some explaining about the consequences of being disobedient and lying. After physically punishing him, Cosby said he asked his son if he had got the point across about never lying. The boy replied, "Yes," and was

*The show was billed as Two Friends. Bill Cosby and Sammy Davis Jr., world's greatest variety performer, made it to New York City's Broadway together and couldn't conceal their joy.*

assured that the punishment had ended. But as the youngster started to exit the barn in tears, Cosby said he hit him again. When the youngster looked at him in disbelief, Cosby told him, "I lied. Do you want me to lie to you again?" The son said, "No." It was the moment of truth and Cosby eloquently describes the encounter in details in his book, *Fatherhood*.

Cosby said the punishment lasted for nearly two years. Then another problem. Cosby said:

"The kid told me that he wanted to be regular people. He said regular people don't go to college, regular

*When Bill Cosby received the 1985 Spingarn Medal from the NAACP in New York City, one of first friends to congratulate him was Greyhound Senior Vice President Joe Black. After receiving an honorary doctorate degree in 1986 from Spelman College, Cosby posed with President Donald Stewart.*

Central State University President Arthur Thomas congratulates Cosby after conferring an honorary doctorate degree upon him. At right, Cosby accepts honorary doctorate degree from Temple University President Peter J. Liacouras in 1982.

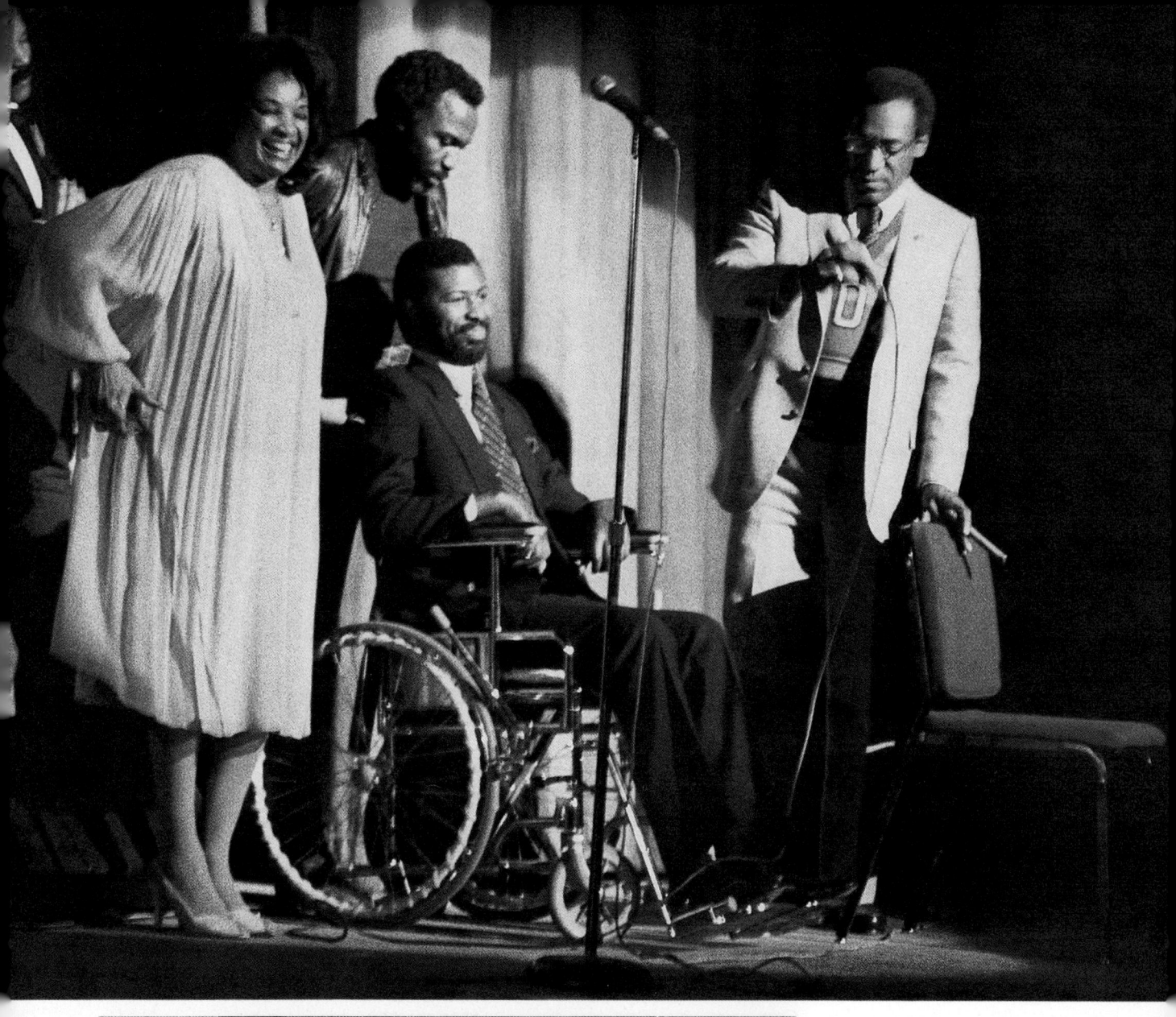

Big-hearted Bill Cosby never forgets friends and worthy causes. When singer Teddy Pendergrass made one of his rare public appearances after suffering paralysis from an auto accident, Cosby introduced him to Philadelphia fans. In Atlantic City, he accepts a check for the UNCF from Ordway P. Burden. Cosby joins Mrs. Rachel Robinson, who heads foundation named for her late husband Jackie Robinson, a baseball Hall of Famer. Cosby was emcee of the program where the 1982 Robie Award was presented to George Weissman, chairman of board of Philip Morris.

123

*After 1979 ceremonies which immortalized him with a star placed on Hollywood's Walk Of Fame, Bill Cosby and wife Camille delight in the symbol that assures Cosby's fame is lasting.*

*In memorable moments attesting to his success as an extraordinary entertainer, Cosby varies his reactions. After receiving the Emmy Award in 1966 as best actor for role in* I Spy, *Cosby gushes with glee as wife Camille congratulates him with a kiss. In 1968, he poses with Lucille Ball as he accepts his third consecutive Emmy Award for his* I Spy *role. Upon receiving Golden Apple Award in 1967 at Women's Press Club in Hollywood, Cosby smiles with Dorothy Malone. At Capital Press Club in Washington, D.C., Cosby relishes award he and* I Spy *co-star Robert Culp received from club's officers President Larry Still (left), former* JET *Washington editor, and Percell Johnson. At NARA Convention in Atlanta in 1967, Cosby was especially delighted to be honored for his* I Spy *role since the award was presented by his cousin, Del Shields, who was a popular Philadelphia radio disc jockey who helped launch Cosby's career.*

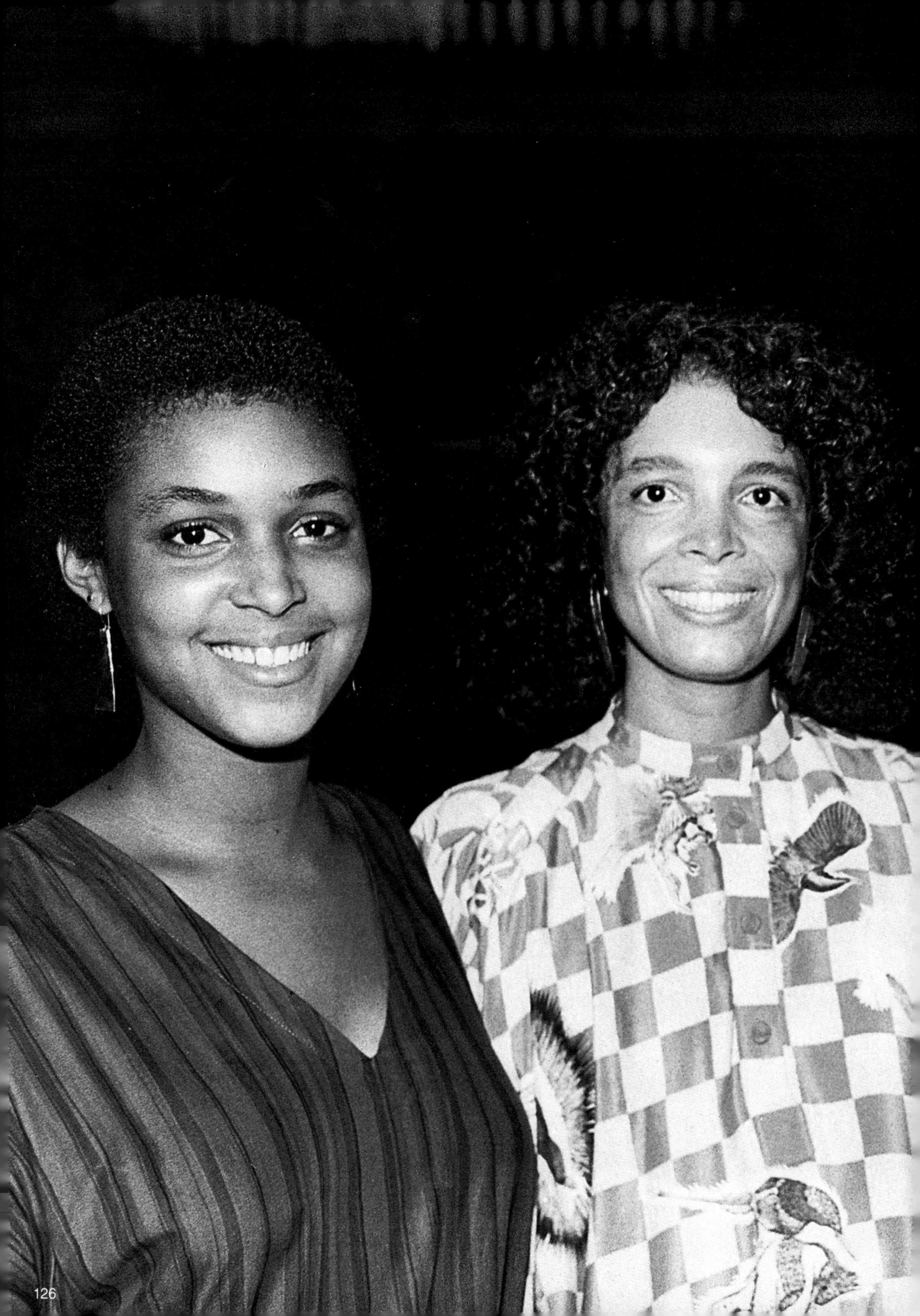

*In 1979 after Bill Cosby's name had been placed on Hollywood's Walk of Fame, Camille poses with three of their children (left to right) Erika, Ennis and Erinn.*

*Dr. Huxtable (Cosby) has a discussion with his children (l-r) Theo (Malcom-Jamal Warner), Denise (Lisa Bonet) and Vanessa (Tempestt Bledsoe).*

*Elvin (Geoffrey Owens) is told by Dr. Huxtable (Cosby) how to please his daughter, Sondra (Sabrina LeBeauf).*

people don't want to be anything important; they just want a regular job. They don't want to be rich, just a regular apartment with a regular car. He said regular people don't want to be a doctor or a lawyer or anything like that.'

This encounter toughened Cosby's stance. He told his son of a resolve made by Camille and him:

"Your mother and I made a list of what regular people do and what regular people don't do. So, you are going to do your own laundry and iron your own clothes because regular people don't have a maid to do their laundry. You are going to make up your own bed and put your own clean sheets on every day because regular people don't have a maid to do that stuff for them. You are going to buff your own floors and do it at the same times of demands of the building because we have certain rules about cleanliness.

"On top of that you will eat a home cooked meal only when your mother cooks because regular people eat their mother's cooking or they have to cook for themselves... Regular people cannot call their girlfriend in Minneapolis because regular people don't live in Massachusetts and have a girlfriend in Minnesota... regular people will get a job after school to prepare for working in a regular job..."

Cosby said that he further told his son that at some point he would take him to Boston and go into the lower economic neighborhoods and tell the

*Dr. Huxtable tries to coach daughter, Sondra, to favor new date who plans to study medicine.*

*Members of The Cosby Show cast are (front, left to right) Lisa Bonet, Bill Cosby, Keshia Knight Pulliam, Phylicia Rashad, (Back, left to right) Tempestt Bledsoe, Sabrina LeBeauf and Malcolm-Jamal Warner.*

*After Cosby instructed his writers to include Sabrina Le Beauf in more of* The Cosby Show *episodes as Sondra, the actress exhibited real talent on the popular NBC show.*

people what his son thinks regular people happen to be and why he wants to be regular people.

"Then I've got to get you out of there right away," he said he told his son, "because I think those people are going to come after your little behind and want to rip the flesh off it, and quite a few of them are going to say, 'Why don't you take my place down here and I'll go live with your folks.' So I think that regular people is going through a little change now.

"My wife said regular people came to her and explained that regular people did not want to be regular people anymore."

Before he left Atlanta during the celebration of the first national holiday in observance of the birthday of Dr. Martin Luther King Jr., the famous entertainer/philanthrophist made a $50,000 gift to Morehouse and then presented Spelman with a $50,000 gift.

"The children that Camille and I have are lining up like airplanes at the ramp," he said. "They are just about ready when one takes off one after the other."

Cosby says that he and Camille have not been cautious in rearing their children as offsprings of the rich and famous. He falls back on his own experience for guidance. "I've lived with poor children," he says of growing up in Philadelphia with his brothers, "but this is the first time I've ever lived with rich children," he quips.

The famous entertainer, while on location in Los Angeles where he had just finished filming a Jell-O commercial when he was interviewed in 1983, said he has to be tough on his five children because they don't live like regular people and he believes regular people would like to live like them. They have to be taught how to live in the real world and he feels it is his primary responsibility to do the teaching and educating.

That is one of the reasons he took some time out of his entertainment schedule to earn the highest academic

*On the NBC set in Brooklyn, talented Tempestt Bledsoe is a source of pride for Cosby, who cast the daughter of two Chicago public school teachers, in the role of Vanessa.*

*In NBC-TV's situation comedy,* The Cosby Show, *the role of an obstetrician is played by Bill Cosby with a wife and five children. The youngest is Rudy, who is portrayed by young actress Keshia Knight Pulliam.*

degree in education from the University of Massachusetts.

"I didn't get that degree to have something to fall back on," the millionaire entertainer stated. He said the degree is a teaching tool to use at home and wherever he encounters young people.

He has no plans to teach. "In terms of education," Cosby said "It doesn't mean that I'm going to go into the classroom and work." But his "Fat Albert" TV cartoon series is an effective teaching tool. "That "Fat Albert" is what it is because of my education... The things that I studied, the things that I had to say go into what "Fat Albert" is." He added: "The things that I studied, the things that I had to say go into what I've done with the Electric Company. It goes into what I've done in public speeches, public service announcements; it goes into what I say whenever I talk to young people, whenever I deal with parents of children. That is what it is all about."

He said all of the education and experiences are invaluable in dealing with his children.

As far as their being Cosby children whose parents are multi-millionaires, he responds: "Well, I would hope that they

*Talented Malcolm-Jamal Warner plays the role of Theo, the only son of the TV Huxtables, whose household head is played by Cosby.*

*Disappointed and dejected after he finds out that his son doesn't have the potential of Walter Payton, football's greatest running back of the champion Chicago Bears, Dr. Huxtable (Cosby) is consoled by wife Clair (Phylicia) in the NBC-TV episode, "Is That My Boy?"*

would not cry about it. I hope that my children would be strong enough from my teachings, my wife's teachings that they would recognize an idiot when they see one and not be offended by a person who has a low-class attitude. And I don't want them to excuse these people...

"Of course you know you have peer pressures, but I told Erica and Erinn, I really don't think that the person who will get after you or want to pick on you or hurt your feelings because you seem to have more than they would make a good friend. Now, if you want to get them off your back and you don't want to be a squealer or anything like that, then just simply tell them to go and get lost.

"We don't believe in turning cheeks, man. We don't believe in loving people who act dumb. We believe in telling them point blank, 'Don't bother me. Go some place else,' because the older you get the more you are going to see it."

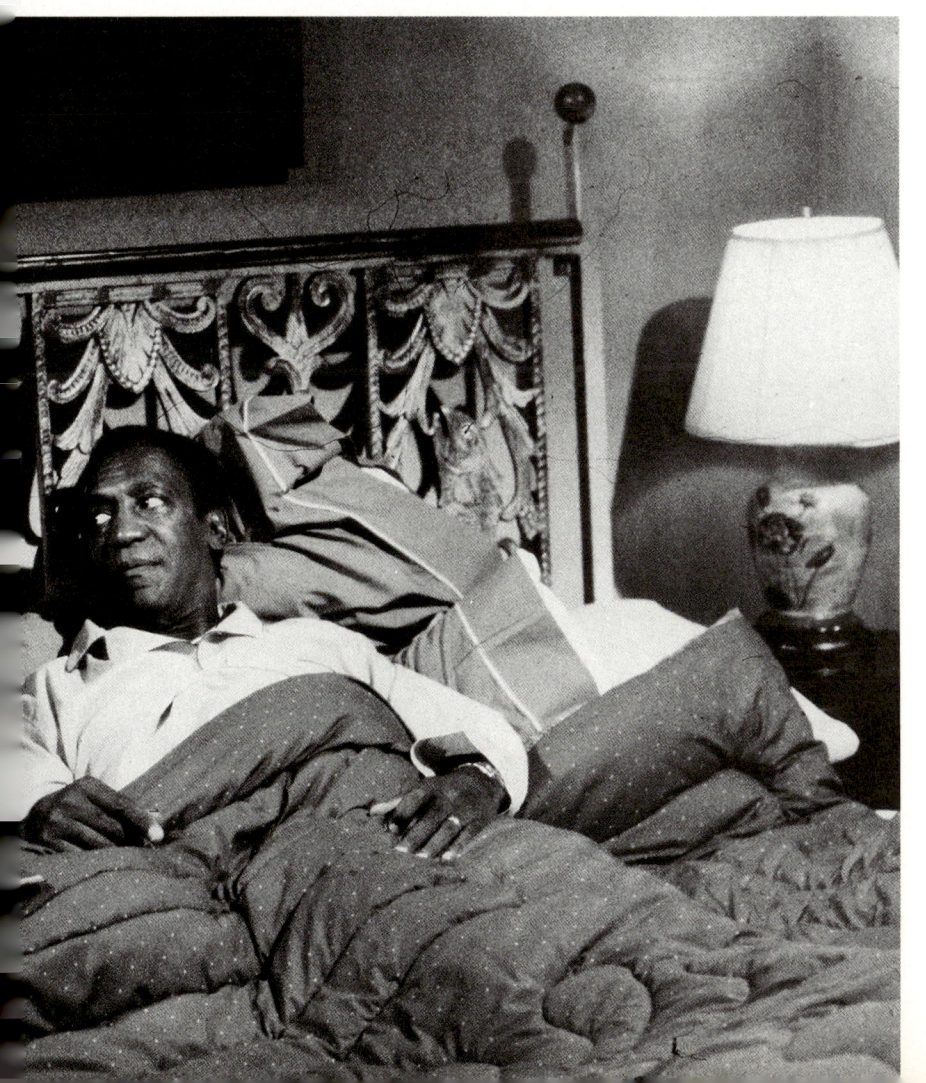

*With their children retired for the night, Cosby's expressive eyes telegraph the thoughts the writers penned for his bedroom encounter with Rashad during the taping of his top-rated TV show*

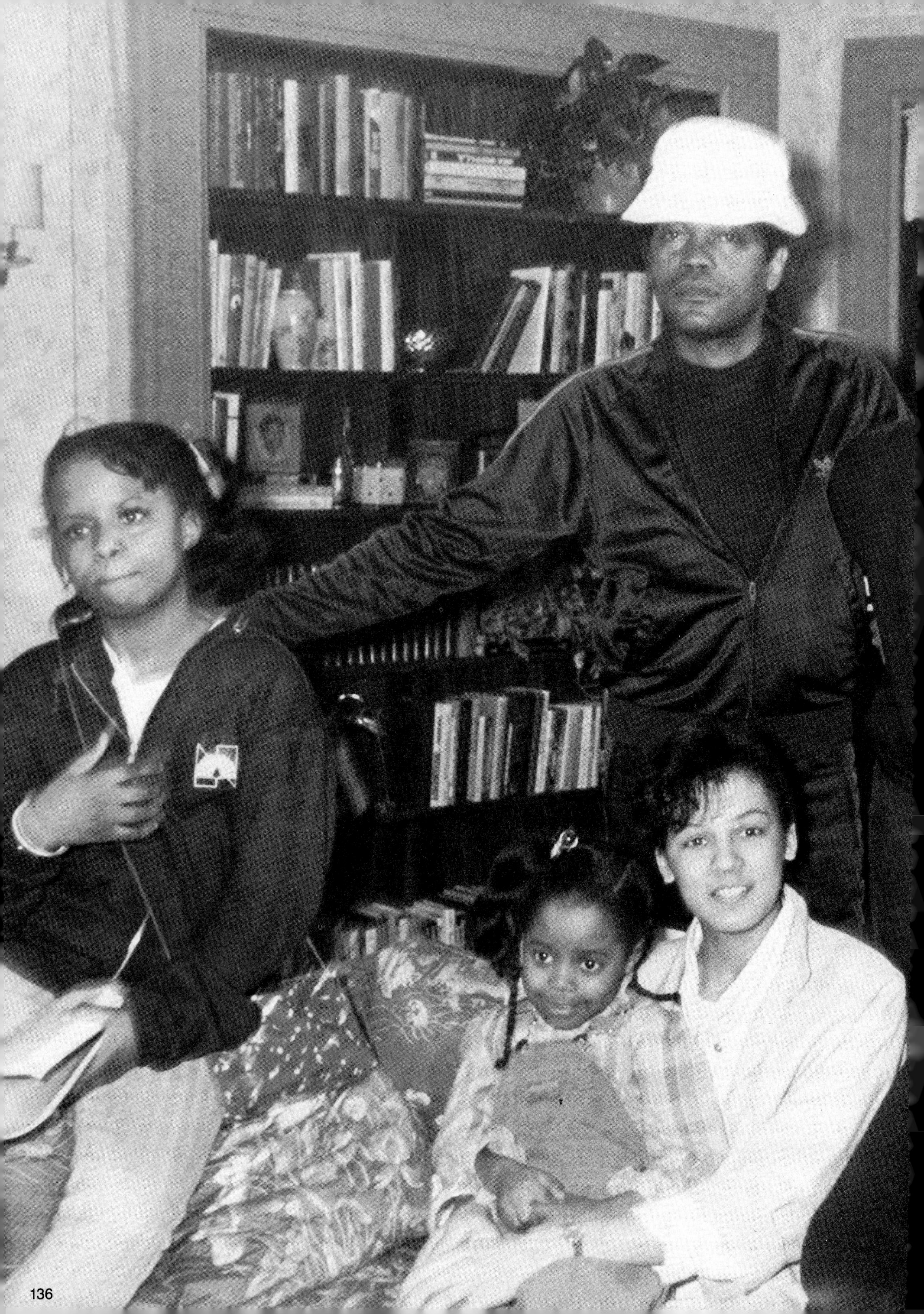

*After taping a TV segment with legendary singer/actress Lena Horne as guest star, The Cosby Show cast and staff members are captured in a candid photo with her. Shown (front, left to right) are Tempestt Bledsoe, Keshia Knight Pulliam, Sabrina LeBeauf, Lena Horne and Phylicia Rashad. Standing (l-r) are actor Clarence Williams, Malcolm-Jamal Warner, Jay Sandrich, Bill Cosby and Lisa Bonet.*

*Cosby, in his role of Dr. Cliff Huxtable, tapes a segment that features Stevie Wonder. Cast members are (left to right) Phylicia Rashad, Keshia Knight Pulliam, Tempestt Bledsoe, Malcolm-Jamal Warner and Lisa Bonet.*

Even though he is a celebrated person whose *The Cosby Show* shot to the No. 1 position in the regular and rerun seasons for 1984-86 and began the 1986-87 season cemented in the same No. 1 position, Cosby doesn't believe that famous actors, athletes and entertainers have to be paraded in lower economic neighborhoods like the one where he grew up to give the children positive images.

*Cosby coaxed singer Joe Williams into accepting a role on* The Cosby Show *as father of Clair Huxtable, whose character is played by Phylicia Rashad.*

"The kids see these people, see how well they live and then that is what they want to be, and I said I don't expect that. I said, 'Have you ever bothered to look at your mother who cooks your breakfast, gets on the bus, rides to clean somebody's house, comes back, does your dinner, gives you money so you can buy some records or a stereo?' I said, 'Tell me that that is not a positive image. Tell me that your father who comes home and changes clothes to

139

*The Huxtables entertain Cliff's (Cosby) parents before taking them to a restaurant to celebrate parents' wedding anniversary. Cosby says he loves to see families dining in a restaurant and going to church.*

go to his second job to support you working 18 hours a day—is not a positive image...' The image is sitting right there in your home. Forget about the celebrities. We're not gods; we're not perfect people and we have our problems."

Some of the problems facing Cosby and Camille revolve around how to make the best use of their money and time to fight for Black causes. They couldn't resist the siren songs of Black causes and now they are paying the price for their involvement.

They first got involved as contributors to Black organizations and their causes more than two decades ago when Cosby, accompanied by his *I Spy* series co-star, Robert Culp, would travel from Hollywood to Chicago to help Rev. Jesse Jackson launch Operation Breadbasket, the economic division of Southern Christian Leadership Conference (SCLC), then led by Dr. Martin Luther King, Jr.

After Dr. King was assassinated on April 4, 1968, Jackson later quit SCLC and organized Operation PUSH, but Cosby continued to support Jackson.

Today, the Cosbys are still fighting for Black causes because of Reaganomics —hard times of joblessness, cutbacks in social programs and increased spending for defense brought on by the policies of President Ronald Reagan's Administration.

"When it was said that Ronald Reagan was going to be in office, I said to Camille, 'We're going to have to double up on the amount of money that we are giving to certain organizations because things are going to be cut back and all these people are going to look for the entertainers to give them a hand,'" the philosophical philanthropist told this writer during an interview for a cover story that featured him and his wife on the cover of JET (May 31, 1982).

The couple had helped raise $337,000 for PUSH at a testimonial for Rev. Jackson, then president of the Chicago-based organization of People United To Save Humanity.

Assessing the plight of Blacks at that time, Cosby said, "Just leave the door open and you can be there for two weeks with the foundations and people, who want and need, coming through. You will be looking at the United Negro College Fund (UNCF), Jesse Jackson's Excel Program (of which Camille is a board member), Rev. Joseph Lowery and SCLC in Atlanta, the NAACP and its two divisions, Sickle Cell Anemia and voter registration groups. I mean you can just sit down and make a list of about 40 organizations if you need to and want to give some money to them."

Because he believes UNCF is right

*Bill Cosby invited Lena Horne to appear on his TV show and later revealed that he wants to produce a TV series which will star the legendary singer/actress.*

*After his performance at Harrah's in Atlantic City, Bill Cosby and Phylicia Ayers-Allen greet real life and TV family members. Phylicia, singer on the show bill, was congratulated by her mother Vivian Allen and son, Billy, along with Malcolm-Jamal Warner, who plays TV son Theo to Cosby and her on* The Cosby Show.

when its slogan says "A Mind is a terrible thing to waste," Cosby declared, "A higher education has to be the No. 1 priority" on their list of Black causes.

"The second most important thing as far as I am concerned is voting," Cosby says. "It is a shame and a mess that we cannot get our folks out to register and vote."

In his travels across the country to headline benefit performances for Black events, Cosby says that he has observed a "crab in the barrel" attitude toward Black leadership by some of the people who are being helped and need it most. "I remember a time when certain fools took Jesse Jackson to task because Jesse was wearing a pair of shoes that looked kind of expensive." He says those kind of detractors "want to see you look almost a mess and as long as you are suffering, it makes them feel just wonderful—like crabs in a barrel."

In pushing Black causes, Cosby isn't neglecting his family. "I tell my children that I'm going to leave you an awful lot of money, but nobody is getting anything unless you have a formal education and can understand what to do with that money." He teaches them that they will have to protect their money if they want to keep living the lifestyle they now enjoy. "I tell them what singer Sophie Tucker said a long time ago, 'I've been poor and I've been rich—and rich is better!'"

Although Cosby contributes his own money to many Black movements, he also spends a lot of time in additional support of his commitments. An avid tennis fan and better-than-average player, Cosby participates in pro-celebrity tennis tournaments to raise funds for various charities. In 1976, Cosby, then a tennis novice, chartered a private plane from Lake Tahoe, Nev., where he was appearing, so he could play in the first annual JET/American Airlines Celebrity Tennis Matches in San Diego, Calif. The tennis classic, played before 3,000 fans, was staged to benefit the predominantly Black American Tennis Association, then headed by Dr. Clyde Freeman of Washington, D.C. and supported by tennis star Arthur Ashe.

In the years that followed, Cosby continued to participate in the JET/AA tennis classics which also benefitted the United Negro College Fund (UNCF) and other Black causes.

In supporting other worthy actions while he was not appearing regularly in a television series, Cosby didn't neglect his own circumstance. He made show business history in 1983 when he teamed with superstar Sammy Davis, Jr., the world's greatest variety performer, as co-stars of "Two Friends," a night club act that premiered at Harrah's in Lake Tahoe, Nev. They later took their "Two Friends" show to Broadway for further acclaim.

But the summer of 1984 brought another dramatic turning point in Cosby's career, reminiscent of 20 years earlier when NBC-TV announced that he would co-star with Robert Culp in *I Spy.*

At that time, in addition to the *I Spy* series, NBC's five-year contract with him for approximately $15 million stipulated that he work on several specials and develop pilots for other series. His contractual commitments to NBC ended when the network canceled *The Bill Cosby Show* after airing it from September 14, 1969 to August 31, 1971.

This time, after being away from a regular television program for eight years following failures with his own shows on CBS and later on ABC, Cosby was returning to the network where his career in television took off.

Cosby, at 47, was back to discuss a pilot for a new series. He was now a man with impressive entertainment credentials in television, motion pictures, record albums, public speaking, concert and night club performances, the most believable commercials on televison—and a multi-millionaire show businessman.

It was against this background that Cosby explained why he was returning to the tube on a weekly family situation comedy. "*The Bill Cosby Show* will rescue NBC from bottom rung of the ratings ladder and save viewers from

*Appearing at Harrah's in Atlantic City, Bill Cosby poses with wife Camille and his television wife, Phylicia Ayers-Allen, who has since married NBC-TV sportscaster Ahmad Rashad. Phylicia opened Cosby's show as a singer, at the suggestion of Mrs. Cosby, who lauds her singing talents.*

After receiving an honorary doctorate degree from Morehouse College in Atlanta, Bill Cosby chats with his son, Ennis, suggesting that he attend the historically Black college upon high school graduation.

*After conferring (below, left) with production consultant Dr. Alvin Poussaint and stage manager Chuck Vinson, Cosby goes to his New York City home, chats on the phone.*

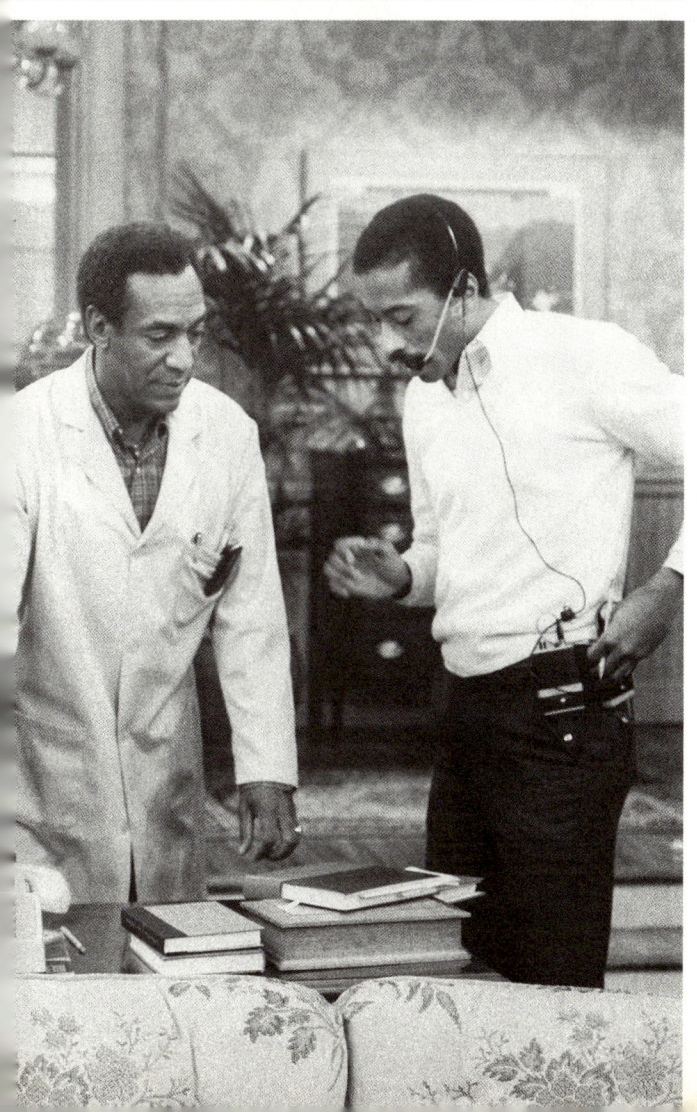

*In his New York City home, Cosby relaxes beneath his favorite painting of wife Camille. Cosby is an art collector and has a treasure of many priceless paintings.*

*At testimonial in Chicago to pay tribute to his pal, Ira Murchison, a former Olympic track champ, Cosby cuts a caper. In Atlanta with wife Camille, the comedian was guest roaster of Arthur Ashe at JET Celebrity Tennis roast.*

what has been described as "a vast wasteland."

As he told this writer for a JET cover story (August 13, 1986), "I watch an awful lot of television and I get a little tired of what I see. If I see one more car roll sideways for two blocks, then there's a guy with a .357 magnum and a hooker with her Black pimp..." He paused, then continued: "We have about six television sets in our house, and it's less expensive for me to do a television series than it is for me to throw them all out." He smiled, tongue in cheek. Although the show would not be strictly autobiographical, Cosby said the cast would bear some resemblance to his wife and five children. He unabashedly admits that he picked a TV wife whose beauty is similar to his real-life wife Camille. He picked actress Phylicia Ayers-Allen to portray his wife and selected for their TV children actresses, Sabrina LeBeau, Lisa Bonet, Tempestt Bledsoe, Keshia Knight Pulliam and actor Malcolm-Jamal Warner.

"My TV wife (now Phylicia Rashad) plays a lawyer and I'm a doctor," Cosby says. "For those of you who have a problem with that, I don't want to hear that's an overload of the Black family, but if you have trouble with a doctor and a lawyer, then that's your problem. It's wherever you grew up, their problem," he allows.

NBC was still somewhat cautious about Cosby and only ordered six

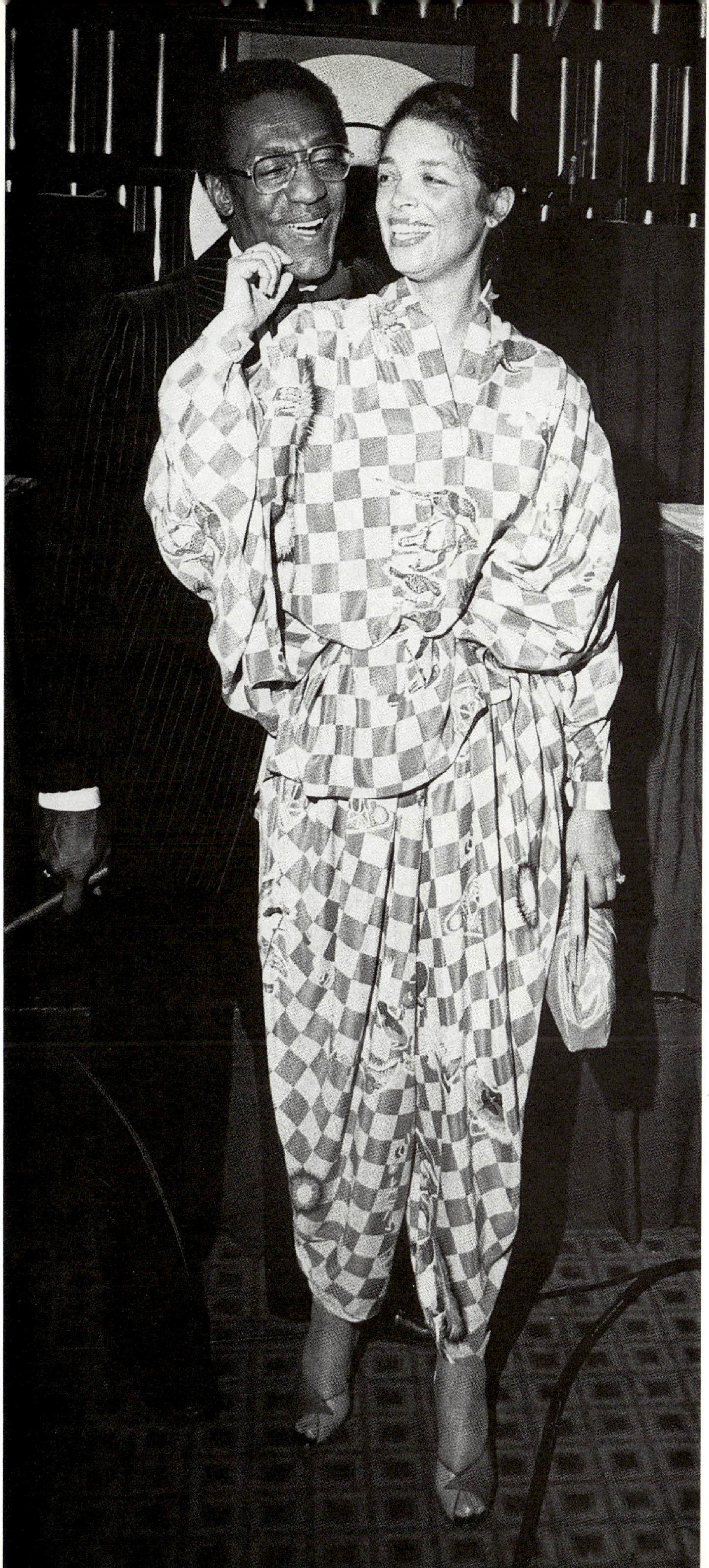

*Cosby clowns with Camille in his dressing room after performing at Harrah's in Atlantic City.*

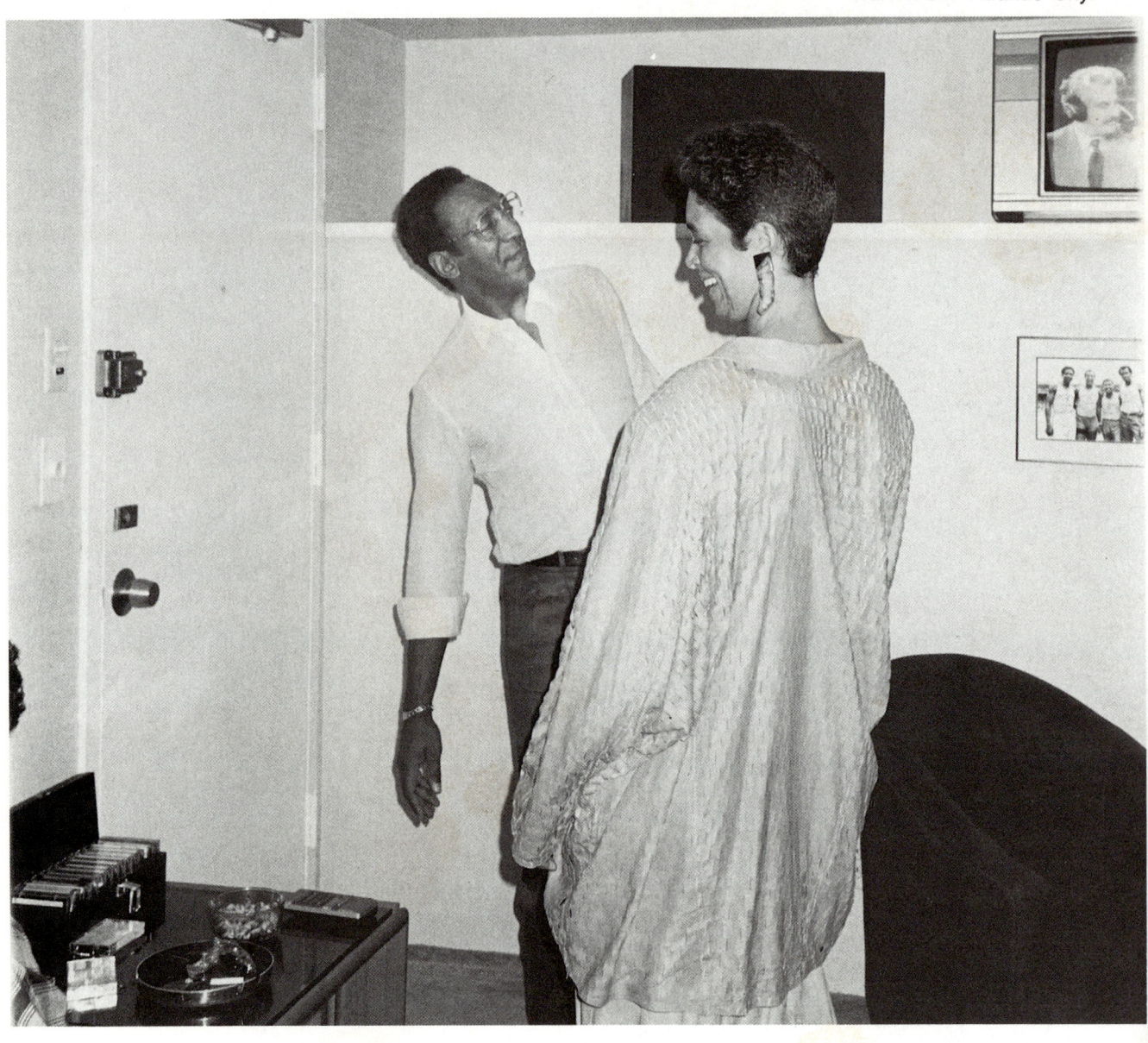

*In New York City, Bill Cosby and wife Camille are enroute to an exhibition of paintings by trumpeter Miles Davis.*

*Sitting in his dressing room at Harrah's in Atlantic City, Bill Cosby discusses a pilot TV program with Tony Orlando, who would have starring role. Camille Cosby listens with interest.*

shows. For the first airing, *The Cosby Show* outdistanced every regular show on television. The stunning showing sent shock waves through the industry. Proving that the sitcom was no fluke, it held on to the No. 1 position in the Nielsen ratings for the remaining five shows.

The success of the show prompted NBC's press department to issue a news release saying: "Bill Cosby's return to series television after an eight-year hiatus has been one of the most phenomenal success stories in the history of the medium. *The Cosby Show* ... was the runaway hit of the 1984-85 season and the highest-rated new series on any network since 1978-79..." NBC's press department also revealed that the sitcom "led the network to a series of stunning victories in the Nielsen ratings. For the season, the series earned a 24.2 rating and a 37 percent share of the audience." For holding down the No. 1 spot in the regular and rerun seasons, *The Cosby Show* won the Emmy Award for Best Comedy Series on television.

In achieving the success, Cosby's character, Dr. Cliff Huxtable, and Phylicia's character, Atty. Clair Huxtable, were saluted as "TV's Top Mom and Dad" in an EBONY cover story dated February 1986. The magazine said that the TV husband and wife are role model parents displaying pride of race and love of family.

"This is a show with a Black American family, but what's important in this show is that our family represents about 90 percent of all people out in the audience," Cosby told the EBONY writer. "We are family and the humor comes out of our attitudes toward each other and life in general. This show," he adds, "will work to show all Americans that if they really love our children, all children are the same the world over."

As real-life father of four daughters and a son, Cosby says Dr. Huxtable and his wife Clair try to maintain realism and give people another choice besides the one that they may make when they are angry.

"If you are a person who sees something happen and you get upset and become verbally abusive, physically abusive, perhaps if you see

*Hosting a Motown TV special at Harlem's Apollo Theater, Bill Cosby introduces Stevie Wonder, who performed.*

*Following wind sprints on a Los Angeles playground, Cosby discusses track techniques that helped him become one of the top track stars at Temple University in the 1960s.*

"There's nobody whom I can be more thankful about than Phylicia," he elaborates as he talks about her role. "I'm happy to go to work because I know I'm going to see her—and it's the same as if you have a good buddy." Emphasizing that the relationship is platonic, Cosby, who says his love for his wife Camille borders on idolatry, says: "The love I have for Phylicia is I'm just happy to be working with her." He says if Phylicia and her NBC sportscaster husband Ahmad Rashad decided to have a baby, the actress can still remain with the show.

Cosby says he is especially pleased with his TV children. His oldest TV daughter, Sondra, is portrayed by actress Sabrina LeBeau, a young college student in real life. On the show, her character Sondra is away in college. He plans to do more with her role. "We haven't worked hard on that," he told JET, "because she is a specialized character." But he has praise for Ms. LeBeauf: "she is a lovely person and a wonderful actress. She's a softer and funnier person but in a straight way. She's not a high comedy actress but if you give her funny lines, she can find a way to straight act and make it funny."

magazine said that the TV husband and wife are role model parents displaying pride of race and love of family.

"This is a show with a Black American family, but what's important in this show is that our family represents about 90 percent of all people out in the audience," Cosby told the EBONY writer. "We are family and the humor comes out of our attitudes toward each other and life in general. This show," he adds, "will work to show all Americans that if they really love our children, all children are the same the world over."

As real-life father of four daughters and a son, Cosby says Dr. Huxtable and his wife Clair try to maintain realism and give people another choice besides the one that they may make when they are angry.

"If you are a person who sees something happen and you get upset and become verbally abusive, physically abusive, perhaps if you see

*Hosting a Motown TV special at Harlem's Apollo Theater, Bill Cosby introduces Stevie Wonder, who performed.*

153

the Huxtables and what happened to them happened to you, then next time you may stop and say 'wait a minute. There's another way to do this other than popping this kid upside the head.' I don't say that hitting a kid will never work," Cosby hastens to add. "And I don't condone that you pop the kid anytime you see it or have the whole neighborhood pop the kid."

Cosby elaborates as he contrasts his TV Huxtable family with his real life family. He said:

"Our shows are funny. They have that wonderful caring, loving feeling storyline." He emphasized that the Huxtable family tries to solve all of their problems without violence or profanity.

"Now in real life," Cosby stated, "I will go off. I do my share of yelling in real life and cursing and hitting, but I also feel that I have a good control before I light on somebody. I also feel that the children understand that when I do get ready, that this is not just an everyday occurrence."

In all of his episodes in the second season, each character in the family grows in responsibility, especially Clair.

In the February interview in EBONY, Cosby says "Clair has been given more to do. She is quite capable of handling comedy on her own—without Cliff. An accomplished actress, Phylicia is... So this year, there's more for her to play with. We're going to work on more emotions for her—things to play with in terms of children and husband.

*Prior to start of 16th edition of U.S. Olympic invitational at Meadowlands Arena in East Rutherford, N.J., actor Bill Cosby takes baton as he runs final leg of his relay race during the taping of his No. 1 TV show for the 1985-86 season.*

*Following wind sprints on a Los Angeles playground, Cosby discusses track techniques that helped him become one of the top track stars at Temple University in the 1960s.*

"There's nobody whom I can be more thankful about than Phylicia," he elaborates as he talks about her role. "I'm happy to go to work because I know I'm going to see her—and it's the same as if you have a good buddy." Emphasizing that the relationship is platonic, Cosby, who says his love for his wife Camille borders on idolatry, says: "The love I have for Phylicia is I'm just happy to be working with her." He says if Phylicia and her NBC sportscaster husband Ahmad Rashad decided to have a baby, the actress can still remain with the show.

Cosby says he is especially pleased with his TV children. His oldest TV daughter, Sondra, is portrayed by actress Sabrina LeBeau, a young college student in real life. On the show, her character Sondra is away in college. He plans to do more with her role. "We haven't worked hard on that," he told JET, "because she is a specialized character." But he has praise for Ms. LeBeauf: "she is a lovely person and a wonderful actress. She's a softer and funnier person but in a straight way. She's not a high comedy actress but if you give her funny lines, she can find a way to straight act and make it funny."

*Called a workaholic by some of his show biz associates, Cosby puts his creative talents to work for his family and the results of his dedication is explained on desk sign.*

The star of TV's No. 1 show not only offered his opinions of Ms. LeBeauf, but gave his views of his other TV children in a JET story (Oct. 7, 1985):

Lisa Bonet, 18-year-old daughter of a teacher in San Francisco, where she was born, portrays Denise. "Now this is a dynamite, natural actress who is going to fool a lot of people this year. She is funny and gives powerful performances. Many times when I look at her, especially with this new haircut,

*Backstage at Fox Theater in Atlanta, Cosby is visited after show by his brother, Russell, and his (Russell's) daughter along with Cole Johnson-Vinion of Chicago.*

Bill Cosby and famed pianist Erroll Garner (above, left) took time from their appearances at the Las Vegas Hilton Hotel for a joint broadcast to Australia and New Zealand. In Los Angeles, Cosby used his cigar like a baton to direct his Bunions Bradford Sextet at Memory Lane Club.

Jazz musician Monk Montgomery listens to Cosby practice as a bassist during the intermission of a Los Angeles nightclub performance. One of his favorite drummers is Art Blakey, who visited him and performed on a segment of the popular The Cosby Show.

*On the set of* The Cosby Show, *Cosby poses with saxophonist Grover Cleveland and Stu Gardner, who produced for Columbia Records* A House Full Of Love — Music From The Cosby Show. *The Columbia recording features some vocals by Cosby, who manages to mix humor with serious messages about love.*

Prof. Barry Beckham of Brown University presents Cosby a book which the actor lauds as helpful to students. Cosby joins Julius "Dr. J" at benefit concert in Philadelphia. Pennsylvania Gov. Dick Thornburgh presents Cosby an award for outstanding achievements in the arts as a Pennsylvanian.

she does remind me facially, if I'm far away and I don't have my glasses on, of a short Camille." Ms. Bonet, who was featured on NBC-TV's *St. Elsewhere,* studied three years at the Celluloid Actor's Studio in North Hollywood.

Malcolm-Jamal Warner, 15, who was born in Jersey City, N.J., but grew up in Los Angeles, portrays Theo, the only boy: "Malcolm is fun to work with. He's thirsty, learns quickly and wants to do his best. He is always prepared and can do comedy. He is very, very intelligent—all of the children (on the show) are very intelligent people." Warner has made guest appearances on *Fame, Matt Houston, Call To Glory, NBC Friday Night Videos* and EBONY/JET *Showcase.*

Tempestt Bledsoe, 12-year-old Chicagoan who attends a school for exceptional children in New York City, is cast as Vanessa: "She's a very bright youngster and we will change her character this year. Of all the actors and actresses that we have, Tempestt will have the most flexible role because each year a different thing will be asked of her and you will be able to see her grow." Bledsoe has been in show biz since she was five and has appeared in numerous commercials.

Keshia Knight Pulliam, 6, who was born in Newark, N.J., portrays Rudy. "She is fun to deal with. We're taking the baby out of her and asking for more maturity in her character because she has the ability to learn quickly and has earned the reputation on the set for rarely flubbing her lines." She has been in show biz almost all of her life. At age eight months, she appeared in several episodes of *Sesame Street* and was in the Motown movie, *The Last Dragon,* which stars singer/actress Vanity and Talmak.

With the success of *The Cosby Show,* which picked up eight nominations for Emmy Awards during the first season, all of the TV networks started checking out the show to see if a similar format would produce similar results.

*In 1969, after he became star of* The Bill Cosby Show *on NBC-TV following the successful* I Spy *detective series, Bill Cosby visited Detroit and accepted an award from Rep. John Conyers (right) and Ted Stringer.*

Cosby was told that Flip Wilson, who was returning to television in a series called *Charlie & Company,* had criticized him. Wilson was quoted as saying: "Cosby's family is bourgeois; we're an average Black family..." Cosby was asked if he thought that was a terrible thing for Wilson to say. "No, I think it is funny," Cosby responded. "I know Flip. Flip is a friend of mine. Flip would not say something like that and mean harm. Flip is a comedian. He came out to say something funny and what he said was funny."

The Chicago *Sun-Times* newspaper on January 17, 1986 carried this headline: "Redd Foxx Cant's Be A Cosby Clone." The writer's story began: "Well, you can certainly say this about Redd Foxx: He's no Bill Cosby."

Both Wilson's new TV series and the new Foxx show floundered and failed in the success shadow of Cosby's No. 1 show in much the same manner as Cosby thrashed about in the wake of the top-rated shows of Wilson and Foxx 15 years ago.

All of a sudden, the label "Cosby clone" was put on nearly every Black

Cosby reacts after receiving the Harvard Lampoon's first ever Lifetime Achievement in Comedy Award, the "Elmer." He accepted the award on the Cambridge, Mass., campus in 1983. In Houston, Tex., Cosby is congratulated by TV anchorman Walter Cronkite and NCAA President James Frank upon receiving the Roosevelt Award. Between shows at Las Vegas Hilton, Cosby accepts Ampex Golden Reel Award from Cher Cunningham for his gold album, Yes, Yes, Yes. While filming a segment of The Cosby Show in his role as Dr. Cliff Huxtable, Cosby accepts People's Choice Award at Los Angeles' Cedars Sinai Hospital, where award was presented. Show host Army Archerd (right) and two unidentified crewman congratulate Cosby.

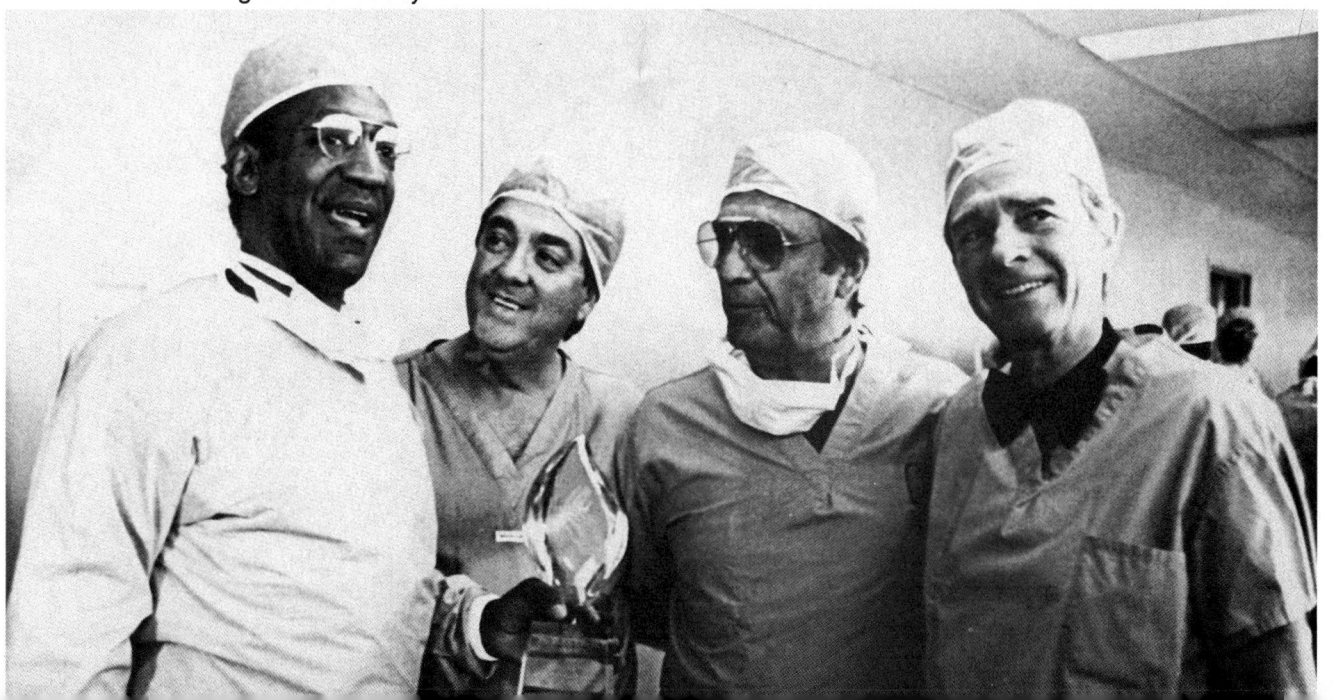

163

*In Chicago, Cosby and Sammy Davis Jr. visited Irv Kupcinet for interview on The Kup TV show. Cosby appeared on David Frost's talk show. He joked with actor Anthony Quinn at a film studio.*

television show on the airwaves, but no fuss was made of White shows with a similar family format as that of *The Cosby Show.*

"And you wonder why?" Cosby asks. He said he would be pleased to have sitcoms measured by his standards. "The formula is very, very simple," he says and then explains: "First, write the story. Then try to be funny. You won't ruin the story, but if you try to be funny while you're doing a story, you're going to forget the line of the story. You're going to forget your point."

Cloning Cosby is not the only controversy that has been fanned by the success of his show. Some critics complain that since *The Cosby Show* has so much crossover appeal, he should deal with more subjects that tackle social problems of Blacks.

When his show began dealing with the problems of courtship by his TV daughters, he was challenged to deal with interracial dating.

He says "these neo-liberals" act as though the image that the Cosby cast projects as a family "has no business being what it is on TV." He told JET during an interview in his New York townhouse about one of his critics:

"A guy said to me, 'Well, at least you won't deal with interracial dating.' I said, Why? He said, 'Well you got Blacks.'" Obviously irritated by what he considers a nitpicking notion, Cosby relates his response:

"If it's an interracial affair, then where

did the White kid come from?" He continues: "It just becomes silly after awhile. I mean, where did the White kid come from? Now, he didn't come from my house. It would be quite interesting to find out what the Caucasian family was doing with the boy instead of bringing him over to my house for our life story. I mean, it's general knowledge that if you have an interracial couple, the baby belongs to the Black people. So actually, there is nothing interracial. That's our child."

He illustrates the point by referring to Daley Thompson, the English decathlon champion who was in the spotlight at the 1984 Los Angeles Olympic Games and had a tryout as an actor. Although

*Not spoiled by success, Cosby visits restaurant in D.C., where he ate as an upcoming comic. He reminiscences with NCNW President Dorothy Height and Mrs. Ben Ali, wife of the owner who poses (below) with Cosby.*

*During the premiere of the 1985 season of EBONY/JET Showcase, Bill Cosby was interviewed by co-host Greg Gumbel at a track in Las Vegas.*

*When EBONY/JET Showcase premiered its 1986 season, Cosby was interviewed by co-host Deborah Crable at Lake Tahoe, Nev. JET West Coast photographer Isaac Sutton posed with Cosby after photographing the star.*

*Dynasty,* I wouldn't be surprised if Sondra (the TV daughter who is away at college) got pregnant and the Huxtables became the people who had to deliver the baby—and we would do a two-part on that," Cosby muses. With his patterned smirk-smile, Cosby flicks ashes from his ever-present cigar and offers more thoughts:

"If they put *Dallas* up against us and *Dynasty,* thinking they would bump us off the air, the Huxtable daughter would get married, become pregnant and have a difficult carriage and the father

168

"Old" Bill Cosby stops in mid-dive to check out a fine young lady who was a model in the December 1980 EBONY, in which he wrote a whimsical article about middle age—and some other aggravations.

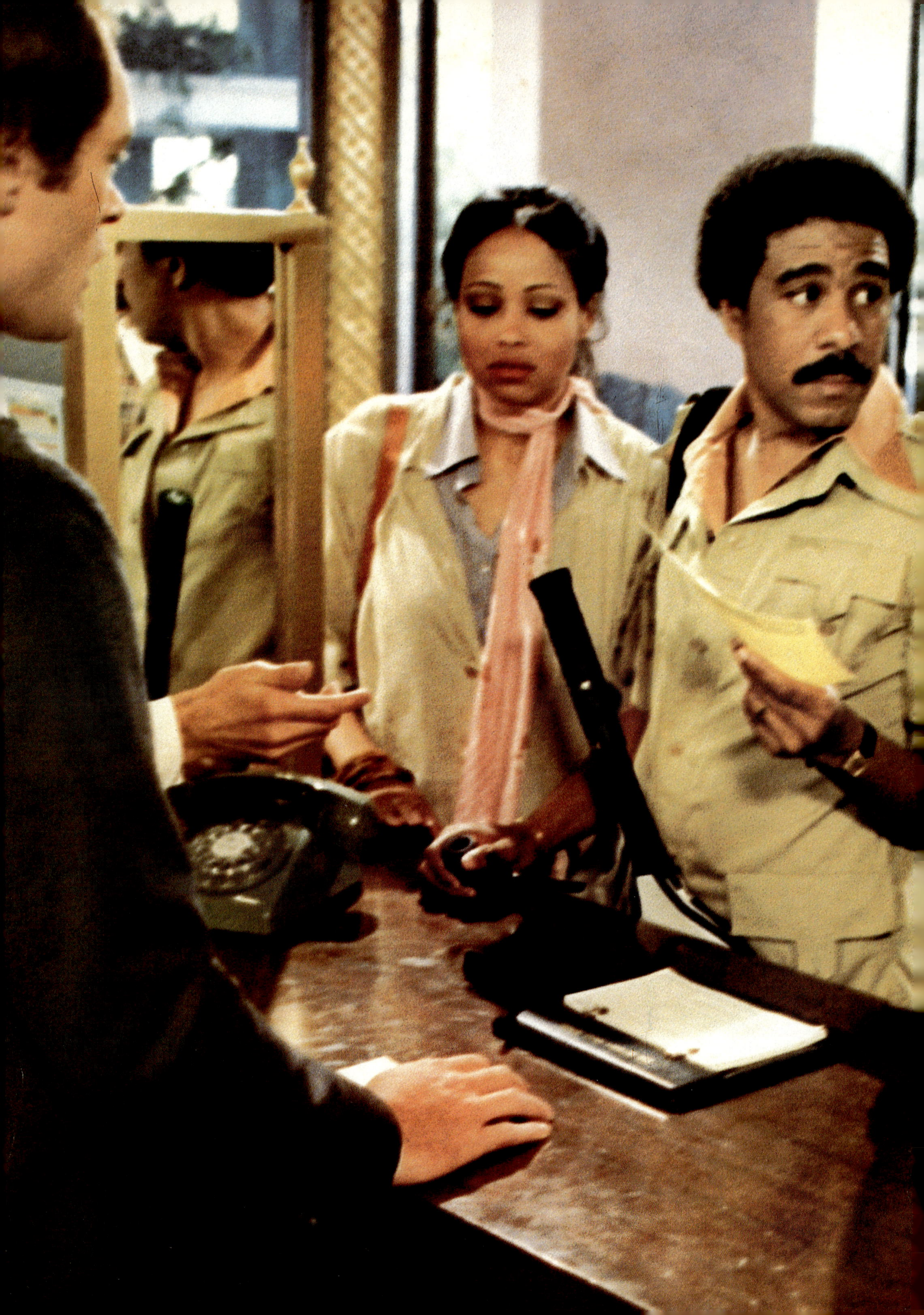

*In 1978, Bill Cosby played his first slapstick comedy role in the film, California Suite, with (left to right) actress Gloria Gifford, actor Richard Pryor and actress Sheila Frazier.*

*An avid athlete who regularly plays tennis, Cosby keeps an eye on his weight. He stands 6 feet 1 and tries to keep the scales at 180 pounds.*

Bill Cosby returned to NBC-TV in 1984 as Dr. Cliff Huxtable in The Cosby Show, which quickly climbed to the top of the ratings as the best weekly situation comedy on television.

Cosby is shown with Keshia Knight Pulliam, who plays his TV daughter, Rudy, on The Cosby Show. *The actress, at age 7, was nominated in 1986 for a TV Emmy as best supporting actress.*

*Bill Cosby booked singer Phylicia Ayers-Allen in 1985 to open his night club show in Atlantic City. She plays his TV wife, Clair Huxtable, and is now married in real life to Ahmad Rashad.*

*In 1985, Bill Cosby appeared on the holiday cover of JET. He was top of a poll as favorite Santa Claus. His TV series, The Cosby Show, also topped all television shows.*

# I L♥VE M♥Y WIFE

Friday, August 8th, 1986

**MENU**

**American-Style Canapes**

Fresh Corn and Maytag Blue Cheese Fritters
Chiles Rellenos Santa Fe Style
Chilled Steamed Mussels stuffed with Curried Tomato Chutney
"Carpetbagger's Fried Chicken"
Cajun-Style Blackened Shrimp Brochettes

*Bill and Camille Cosby arrive at New York's Twenty-Twenty restaurant for his "I Love My Wife" party.*

Oldest daughter, Erika, 21, bestows "I love my dad" kiss upon Cosby's cheek. Erinn, 19, was out of city.

*On festive occasion at Twenty-Twenty restaurant, Bill and Camille Cosby pose with their son, Ennis, 17; daughters, Evin, 9; and Ensa, 13; along with restaurant co-owners Valerie Simpson and Nick Ashford.*

*Attending the "I Love My Wife" fete, Bill Cosby's father-in-law Guy Hanks chats with Ronald Crockett (left). Cosby engages in conversation with his mother-in-law Mrs. Hanks (right) and Mrs. Arlene Howard.*

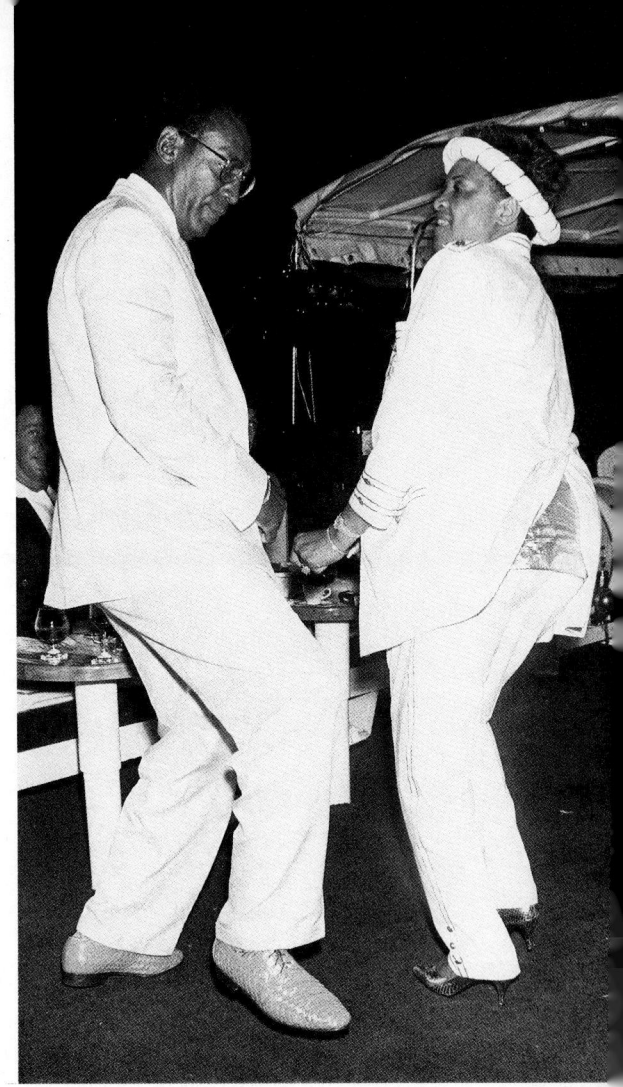

*Aboard the yacht Entrepreneur in New York City, Cosby cuts capers with radio personality Mary Mason, then sits and engages in chitchat with (left to right) Josephine Premice, Camille and Mrs. Gladys Rogers.*

(his Dr. Huxtable TV character) would have to make a decision whether he was going to do it or let someone else do it — or could he stand to deliver his first grandchild?

"But that's only just in case. I want everybody to know that if we wanted to get up and try to get some kind of outlandish ratings, we're capable of thinking of things like that," he allows.

Admittedly proud of the new acclaim that results from the success of his show, Cosby talks of some of the changes he sees in reaction to him now. He observes:

"Now the cats come up to me and tell me that I'm the funniest man in the world. I said, no thank you. I don't want that title. I'm not in competition with anyone... Just tell me, man, you make me laugh... I never got into this business to be measured against somebody... Now, all of a sudden I'm the funniest man in the world. Two months from now, somebody else will be the funniest man in the world."

Cosby, who has Emmys and Grammys, has removed himself from competing against his fellow actors and comedians, but he forsees a problem ahead. He explains:

"Camille is in the studio producing, editing my comedy album for Warner Brothers. Well, Camille has been in the studio about a week working on this comedy album, coming in sometimes at two or three o'clock in the morning. When the album comes out, the record company will want to go for a Grammy. Now, I think my wife would like to win a Grammy for it... I'm going to have a problem this time if Camille wants it to be a Grammy winner because of her hard work in the studio."

*Bill Cosby made show biz history in 1986 when he broke all records in the 54 years of New York City's Radio City Music Hall. His 15 shows grossed $2.8 million, surpassing pianist/singer Liberace, who grossed $2.4 million in 21 shows.*

*Cosby responds after receiving 1985 NAACP Spingarn Medal in New York, where he was congratulated by Lena Horne NAACP Executive Director Ben Hooks. Cosby is a longtime supporter of the Black organization and its goal of an open society with equal opportunities.*

As this EBONY/JET Special Issue goes to press, Bill Cosby is the most celebrated personality in the whole world of television and he made this assessment of himself:

"In the position that I'm in, I have climbed over a tremendous number of people of all colors. And when I look at the position I'm in and look at those other people, the thing that I know is that I have more than these people. Even if I didn't make as much money, there was no way they could have topped me.

"I know that from my drive and my spirit and what I want, there is no way that I would be on that corner drinking wine with the cats my age. There is no way. I'm not going to accept that.

"There is no way that I am not going to vote. There is no way that I'm not going to work two to three jobs to make sure that my children go to college.

"I mean that was set in my life and in my life's plan. I'm not interested in what happens next door or whose got a bigger car or anything like that...

"Now because I'm a millionaire, that makes me a Sophie Tucker—(as she says) 'I've been poor and I've been rich and rich is better.'"

With his unprecedented fame and his uncalculated fortune, one could ask, what's ahead for Bill Cosby?

185

**BILL COSBY TELLS NEED FOR BLACK HEROES**

In 1967, after he won his second Emmy Award for Outstanding Performance by an Actor in a Leading Role in a Dramatic Series, *I Spy,* Bill Cosby appeared on the cover of JET (Oct. 19, 1967) and wrote a by-line feature, telling the need for Black heroes.

Using JET as a forum to explain why he wants to better the image of Blacks, who were then called Negroes, Cosby's by-line feature appeared in JET by permission of Times-Post Service. Cosby writes:

"One of the basic problems of the Negro in America today is that of identification. As children we all found our heroes in the characters brought to us by the mass media, but up to now all the respectable roles have been dealt out to the White man. This is not meant to deride White heroes.

"As a child I loved Humphrey Bogart and Spencer Tracy and Roy Rogers, but I didn't have any Negro heroes to identify with. I, of course, enjoyed the Black performers sent over the air waves—the Amos 'n' Andys, the Willie Bests and the Rochesters—but these were to be laughed at, not emulated. This was pretty much an accepted thing when I was a child, but today, since the Black man has gained self-pride, it can no longer be accepted.

"The importance of a self-image must not be underestimated. The picture you present to the world is only a reflection of the picture you have of yourself. The more you think you are capable of, the more you try to achieve. Then where is the Black child supposed to find his Black heroes? The child living in the ghetto goes to school and has a teacher who urges him to continue his studies so he can improve himself. This is fine.

"The teacher is a possible source of identification. But the child is only in school five hours a day, while the other 19 hours and the weekends are spent in the home and on the streets of the ghetto. Here the dope peddler and the pimps wear diamond rings and drive flashy cars. They impress the kids with their money and their worldly wisdom because they have found a way to beat the system.

"The parents of these children, in most cases, are financial failures manifested by the fact that they are still living in the ghetto. Those Negroes who have made successes of themselves, those who struggled to become doctors, lawyers, etc., and who would be desirable sources of identification have moved out of the ghetto (their reason for struggling). Therefore, the image of these hardworking, ambitious, successful Black men is lost to the ghetto children. Then where can the Black child find a desirable image? The answer must lie with mass media. It is the responsibility of TV and films to build a better image for the Negro. (I use the strong word "responsibility" because the Black man's problem in this country, and this country's problem with the Black man, will not be alleviated until his self-image improves.)

"I see no reason why there can't be films with Negro cowboys who can shoot and ride and do all those things that people respect in a cowboy. Why can't there be Black pilots in war stories? Why couldn't one of the sketches in the recent film *A Guide For the Married Man* be about a Black couple (not because they are Black, but merely because they are a couple?)

"Certainly Hollywood has been making films lately starring Black actors, but the "Blackness" of the character is always the cause of the conflict in the story. Writers and producers seem to think that you need a special reason for a role to be played by a Negro—that he has to pounce on someone or be pounced on.

"Because of this, Hollywood has helped promote a negative image of the Black man. When a Negro comes on the screen the audience immediately tenses up. They know they are about to witness some violence whether physical, verbal or emotional. If someone were to make a film about a Negro who didn't have any great conflict because of his color, who loved and was loved by a Black girl and raised a Black family, the audience would come back to see it again, looking for some hidden meaning.

"Hollywood so far has been afraid to star Black actors in ordinary roles which don't call specifically for a Negro. They have been afraid to chance financial losses at the box offices. But, Hollywood is forgetting the large Negro population in this country that spends money at the movies, and, more importantly, they are forgetting their responsibility as a medium of mass communication.

"I am interested in bettering the Black man's image. I don't want to present him as a Black man, but as a human being. I will not make love to a White woman in a film because that immediately sets up a color conflict. The identification is much warmer and stronger for both White and Black audiences if you remove that conflict. In the Broadway play *Golden Boy* starring Sammy Davis Jr., and in the motion picture *To Sir, With Love* starring Sidney Poitier, the female leads were White girls. This weakens the identification for the audience. When a Black man approaches a White girl, the audience tenses up expecting an explosion. Even if they know there will be no explosion, the tension remains.

"Personally, I want to do comedy—that is what I can do best. I try to keep my humor away from the specific "Black" and make it pertain to the general "human." Likewise, I want to make films and to play not a Negro, but a human being.

"In this goal Hollywood is not really a great help. I come up against the problem, 'who will play opposite Bill Cosby?' What Negro actresses come to mind? First there is Ruby Dee—no, I'm afraid she is a bit older than I am.

"Second, we think of Diahann Carroll—yes, she will do nicely. Now, after this picture I will be in another. Do I play opposite Diahann again? The studios want a name star. Aha, we think of Leslie Uggams—but then what? Do we go back to Diahann or do we put a mustache on Leslie? The problem is clear. Hollywood hasn't built names for Negro actresses. There is a wealth of Negro talent pounding on closed doors.

"My plan of attack is simple. I am producing a film called *Busman's Holiday* in which I play the main character. The character happens to be Black because I happen to be Black, but that is as far as it goes.

"There will be no KKK, no bigots, no name-calling, no riots. The character will have Black girl friends as Black men usually do. The story will have a conflict because that is necessary to a good story, but the conflict will not pertain to the character's color.

"His conflict will be with himself and with society, not as a Negro, but as a human being. I hope it will be the beginning of a new identity for the Black people in this country."

If life begins at 40, Cosby is only nine years old. Therefore, with the possibility of having decades of living ahead of him, there is no end to the speculation of what he may still accomplish.

But one thing is certain, he will always pick up the telephone or talk in person to JET and EBONY editors to try out a new thought or routine which may later turn up in his night club act, or on a record album or in an episode for his TV show.

For example, as this manuscript was getting ready for the printer, Cosby called this writer, expressing a thought about race relations in America today.

He mused: "If you listen to some bigoted people, those are the people who ask Black Americans to go slow. After 200 years of slavery, one hundred years of fighting and hanging, shooting and covering up, there is a tendency (for bigots) to get the feeling that they believe that we got on the (slave) boat ourselves, that it was our boat and we rowed (from Africa) over here ourselves and said, 'Look, we just want to be a part of this great thing. If you let us stay, we'll work for you free (as slaves) for 500 years!' Now, after 300 years, they (bigots) say, 'Look at them (Black Americans) reneging on the promise they made.''

JET
FAMOUS STARS MAKE BEST COMEDY FILM

JET
Why BILL COSBY and Wife CAMILLE Fight For Black Causes
Ten Things Women Notice About Men

JET
BILL COSBY RETURNS TO TV IN FAMILY SERIES
PHYLICIA AYERS-ALLEN

20c
JET
NEGRO HEROES: REVEALING REPORT ON BEST FIGHTING TEAM IN VIET WAR
BILL COSBY
NANCY WILSON
BILL COSBY FINALLY MAKES LOVE IN '1 SPY'

OCT. 27, 1977/75c 64060 A JOHNSON PUBLICATION
JET
Blacks Get 'A Piece Of The Action' With Poitier's New Movie

JET
BILL COSBY, SAMMY DAVIS First Time To Headline Club Date Together
Preacher Wages 30-Year Fight To Clear Name Of Rape Charge Against Him

JET
BILL COSBY And PHYLICIA AYERS-ALLEN:
Whites Remove Dead From Cemetery Now Owned By Black Man
Book Reveals That Marvin Gaye Feared He Would Turn Gay

20c
JET
STORY BEHIND NEGRO'S VICTORY IN CLEVELAND'S MAYORAL BID
OCT. 19, 1967
BILL COSBY: TV star talks of black peoples' need to identify with black heroes
BILL COSBY TELLS NEED FOR BLACK HEROES

JET
COSBY MAKES MILLIONS TEACHING MANNERS AND MORAL LESSONS ON TV
BILL COSBY

JET
BILL COSBY Tells Why He Is Tough On His Children

JET
BILL COSBY'S TV Children: How He Views Each Of Them
Famous Black Athletes Encouraged To Remember Their 'Racial Roots'
Prince's Proteges Climb Ladder Of Success In Music

JET
Uptown Saturday Night: Hilarious New Black Movie

JET
Bill Cosby Bears Secret Of Success —His Wife

JET
BILL COSBY Plays Santa To Needy Children

JET
BILL COSBY'S Book, 'Fatherhood,' Reveals Why He Is TV's Top Dad
Celebrities Talk About Their Dads On Father's Day
New Census Report Says Blacks Live Longer, Hold Better Jobs, Own More Homes

## The Principles Behind The EBONY/JET Special Issue

**ROBERT E. JOHNSON**

Robert E. Johnson, journalist, is Associate Publisher and Executive Editor of JET. Born in Montgomery, Alabama, Johnson is a graduate of Morehouse College (B.A., Sociology, 1948) and Syracuse University (M.A., Journalism, 1952.) He joined the JET staff in February 1953. Johnson is a member of Sigma Delta Chi Journalism Fraternity, The Society of Professional Journalists, The National Association of Black Journalists, Alpha Kappa Delta National Honorary Sociology Society and Alpha Phi Alpha Fraternity. Johnson is also listed in *Who's Who in Black America*, *Who's Who*, *Who's Who in the Midwest* and *International Biographical Dictionary*. Morehouse College has awarded him the honorary L.H.D. (Doctor of Humane Letters). Miles College and Texas College have awarded him the Litt.D. (Doctor of Letters). In September 1979, he accompanied U.S. Ambassador to the United Nations Andrew Young on President Jimmy Carter's special trade mission tour of Africa, which included Liberia, Ivory Coast, Nigeria, Cameroon, Kenya, Tanzania, Uganda and Senegal. He and his wife Naomi have three children: Bobbye LaVerne Johnson, Attorney Janet Johnson-Vinion and Robert III.

**Norman L. Hunter**

Norman L. Hunter, graphic artist, is Art Director of EBONY/JET. He is also Artist-Designer for Fashion Fair Cosmetics, Supreme Beauty Products (both divisions of Johnson Publishing Company, Inc.,) and for the JPC Book Division. Born in Birmingham, Alabama and reared in Detroit, Hunter is an alumnus of the Art Institute of Chicago and studied at the Society of Arts and Crafts in Detroit. Since he joined Johnson Publishing Company in 1955, he has designed among others, nine books by EBONY Senior Editor Lerone Bennett Jr., and designed the highly successful three-volume set of books, EBONY Pictorial History of Black America (1972). Also a photographer, his work appears often in JET and EBONY. His layouts and designs have won the CEBA Award for a number of consecutive years, and the NNPA Merit Award for Best Typography and Makeup and the Printers Industry Award. In his spare time, Hunter paints. He and wife Claudia are the parents of two sons, Kim Derek and Marc Cedric.

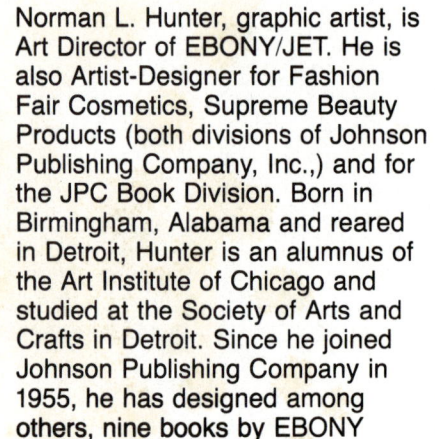

**Sylvia P. Flanagan**

Sylvia P. Flanagan, journalist, is Senior Staff Editor of JET. Born in Chicago, Ms. Flanagan is a graduate of Chicago State University (B.A., Journalism) and Roosevelt University (M.S., Journalism). She is the first Black female to graduate with "honors" in journalism from Roosevelt. A member of JET's editorial staff since 1972, Ms. Flanagan directs JET's photo coverage, serves as talent coordinator for EBONY/JET *Showcase* and EBONY's *American Black Achievement Awards* TV show. She has been editor of "JET's Top 20" record charts since 1973, and established JET's new weekly feature page, "Movies To See." Ms. Flanagan has written stories for JET and EBONY. She is a member of The National Association of Black Journalists, The Chicago Association of Black Journalists and a lifetime member of the NAACP. She was appointed by the president of Carson Pirie Scott to the advisory board of Corporate Level of the department store in Chicago.

**Moneta Sleet, Jr.**

Moneta Sleet, Jr., photographer, is a staff photographer for EBONY, JET and EM magazines. He has traveled on assignments over most of the United States and to Africa, Europe, South America and the West Indies. Born in Owensboro, Kentucky, he is a graduate of Kentucky State College (B.A., business administration, 1947) and New York University (M.A., journalism, 1950). He also attended the School of Modern Photography in New York and Columbia University. He joined Johnson Publishing Company in November 1955. In 1969 he received the Pulitzer Prize in Feature Photography for his photograph of Mrs. Martin L. King, Jr. and her daughter, Bernice, at the funeral of her slain civil rights leader husband. He is a member of the Black Academy of Arts and Letters and has had his works exhibited in the New York Public Library and the Detroit Public Library. He and his wife Juanita, have three children: Gregory, Michael and Lisa.

# ACKNOWLEDGMENTS

The author, in putting this publication together, drew upon the help and resources of a lot of people. Photographs used in Bill Cosby: In Word and Pictures were drawn from the Johnson Publishing Company photo files, individual photographers, photo agencies, organizations and institutions. They are credited on this page.

The text was drawn primarily from personal interviews with Bill Cosby by the author and stories about him which have been published in EBONY, JET and Black Stars magazines. The author also culled from our clipping files, magazines and books; viewed television programs, played Cosby's comedy, instrumental and singing albums; viewed motion pictures that featured him; examined documents and press releases about him.

Cosby's best-selling book, Fatherhood; Ronald L. Smith's Cosby, Catherine Latham's Bill Cosby For Real and Bill Adler's The Cosby Wit, which also drew upon JET and EBONY magazines, were read as source material by the author.

Although I alone am responsible for any shortcomings in this publication, I owe a debt to many people, including my wife Nemi; Publisher John H. Johnson; Assistant to the Publisher Linda Johnson Rice; JET Art Director Normal L. Hunter, JET Senior Staff Editor Sylvia P. Flanagan; EBONY Senior Editor Lerone Bennett Jr.; Lewis Lee, assistant artist; JET Photographers Moneta Sleet Jr., Isaac Sutton, Maurice Sorrell, G. Marshall Wilson, James Mitchell, Vandell Cobb and D. Michael Cheers; JET Managing Editor Malcolm West and staff; EBONY Executive Editor Herbert Nipson and staff; Basil Phillips and Carmel E. Tinkchell of the Johnson Publishing Company Book Division; Pamela Cash, Linda R. Hawkins, and Claire A. Davis of Johnson Publishing Company Special Library; Laurnetta Martin of photo library; Atty. June A. Rhinehart, Vice President and General Counsel of Johnson Publishing Company, and her assistant, Atty. Christopher Benson.

## Photographs by:

Rufus Abdullah, Ampex Corporation, Associated Press Laserphoto, Harold Barnett, Bell System Family Theater, Donald G. Black, The Howard Bloom Organization, The Brokaw Company, A. Ace Burgess, Capitol Records, D. Michael Cheers, Vandell Cobb, Columbia Records, CP Wirephoto, Antonio Dickey, Walt Disney Productions, EBONY Magazine, Ford News Department, Monroe Frederick II, Ron Galella, Bill Gillohm, Norman L. Hunter, Bob Johnson, David LeShay, Loew's Hotel—New York, Bob Lucas, Sue Marx, Les McCann, James Mitchell, Morehouse College, William Morris Agency, NBC Photo—Press Department, New Talent Directions, Inc., Leroy Patton, Harmon Perry, Picturepages, Inc., Tony Rhoden, Fred Rosen, Maurice Sorrell, Black Stars, Dick Stone, Spelman College, Isaac Sutton, UPI, Warner Bros., G. Marshall Wilson.

Cosby's first book was written for fun and directed at tennis players. His book, Fatherhood, was written for fun, too, and directed at everyone who has been either a parent or child. Fatherhood sold over 2 million copies in five months, broke records as the fastest best-seller.